Helping YOUNG CHILDREN TO PLAY

TINA BRUCE

Hodder & Stoughton

A MEMBER OF THE HODDER HEADLINE GROUP

Acknowledgement

My deepest thanks to Ian, Hannah and Tom, especially for all the wonderful experiences we have had as a family learning together about play.

Thank you, Tom, for all the trouble you took over the photographs in the book.

Thanks to the children, parents and staff at James Lee Nursery School who were so helpful while Tom Bruce took the photographs.

British Library Cataloguing in Publication Data
A catalogue entry for this title is available from the British Library

ISBN 0 340 655194

First published 1996
Impression number   10 9 8 7 6 5 4 3 2 1
Year   2000 1999 1998 1997 1996

Typeset by Wearset, Boldon, Tyne and Wear.
Printed in Great Britain for Hodder & Stoughton Educational, a division of Hodder Headline Plc, 338 Euston Road, London NW1 3BH by Bath Press

Contents

1

Why is Play Important for Adults and Children?

Play is a resource to be used later in adult life

In different parts of the world and in different cultures, play is encouraged, facilitated, constrained or seen as unimportant.

This chapter examines the way in which childhood play has a long-term impact on adult life. It becomes a resource which can be used in later life to:

> ▶ deal with setbacks and tragedies
> ▶ live a full life
> ▶ make a major contribution to mental and physical health
> ▶ give a sense of well-being and control
> ▶ help make sensitive, sound relationships with people
> ▶ be creative and imaginative

Play is like a reservoir full of water. The deeper the reservoir, the more water can be stored in it, and used during times of drought.

The benefits of childhood play are of lasting impact during adult life, both through good and bad times. This is how Ida Rentoul Outhwaite (1928, p. 86) in her children's book, describes play, and the ideas, feelings and relationships that are deepened through it, and remain in adult life. The character, Blossom, is sad because her childhood friend Patrick is leaving and growing out of childhood. Maia is Blossom's fairy godmother in the story, who appears whenever Blossom is sad.

Blossom sniffed, 'But it will be different. We shall never have quite the same lovely times again.'

'You will always have them, always,' said Maia. 'Nothing, nothing can ever take them away from you. They are always in the Pool of Memory.'

Sometimes it is easy to see the connection between the child's play and later adult life. The following are examples of well-known people who as children played with wooden blocks, kept their play in the 'pool of memory' and used it later in their working lives.

The writers E.E. Nesbitt and H.E. Wells both played with blocks as children. The poet Robert Louis Stevenson wrote a poem also about blocks. The stories and characters created during blockplay were used later on in novels and poetry. The architect Frank Lloyd Wright played with Froebel's blocks as a child. His architecture is thought by some to resemble blocks.

Childhood play becomes a resource that remains deep inside the maturing person to be used later in adult life.

Play becomes a resource that remains deep inside the maturing person

Children are more likely to be resilient if they have a sense of control and feel they can organise things so that life does not control them (Gotberg, 1995). Children who play are more likely to be children who are resilient and continue to be resilient during adult life, as shown in the chart on page 4.

Play and development

Play is also an important contributor to the all-round development of children.

It helps children to:

> - be whole people
> - be physically healthy
> - be physically co-ordinated
> - be mentally healthy
> - deal with feelings and relationships
> - co-ordinate ideas

Froebel, one of the great pioneers of the importance of play, believed that because of its contribution to development, play is also the most spiritual activity of the child. By this he meant that play helps children to sort out moral matters such as good and evil, justice, right and wrong. Dunn (1988), in her twenty years of observing children in their homes in both the USA and the UK, strongly supports this (see page 6 for further details).

Development is about the general state and direction that the child is taking. Studies of child development used to concentrate almost entirely on biological development. During the 1980s there was more emphasis on the cultural aspects of a child's development. Researchers began to look at the ways children walk, talk and play all over the world. Because of differences across cultures, children do these things in very different ways.

Play and learning

Learning is about being able to do an action by yourself, like jumping on a trampoline, tying a shoelace, or blowing your nose. From the research that has been done on children playing, it seems that play cannot be left to just natural development. If it is, children do not learn to play well. Some researchers believe it is best to teach children directly to play. Others prefer an indirect approach in helping children to play.

Children who are Resilient

▶ feel they are loved
▶ believe their family always will be there when they are really needed
▶ like themselves
▶ have someone they would like to emulate
▶ do endearing things
▶ have a sense of humour
▶ believe in a power greater than seen
▶ believe deep down that things will turn out all right
▶ are willing to try new things
▶ make plans to do things
▶ like to achieve and follow through what they do
▶ can focus on what they are doing and stay with it

Children who Play

▶ feel in control, free to experiment with and transform real life. Play helps children to find ways of making their lives manageable
▶ try out different aspects of family life and try to get things under control
▶ spend this time exploring and working out their relationships with people close to them
▶ experiment with pretending to be different people, particularly role models but also people they fear or dislike
▶ by experimenting with being a baddie or a goodie, find out in a safe way, free from real life, how people feel or behave or react when people are nice to others, or make themselves disliked
▶ relate to larger questions of life: goodness, evil and justice for example. In their play children use these ideas and thus play helps them to think deeply about these concepts
▶ are helped through emotional pain, if they have experienced traumatic situations, for example the children Anna Freud helped to play after they survived concentration camps in Hitler's Nazi Germany
▶ are encouraged in their sense of humour
▶ can have great fun
▶ are encouraged to have good ideas and think creatively as well as feel good and enjoy being together with other children
▶ develop their ability to plan

PHYSICAL

What children do physically can help or hold back their play. Think of all the things that children do as they move about:

> Crawl, step, run, climb, slide, balance, rock, roll, tumble, swing, hop, jump, leap, vault, do handstands and cartwheels, kick, throw, catch, hit and more (Davies, 1995, p. 3).

The child who is physically disabled may find it more challenging to play, and will need careful help from others. Blind children, for example, often find crawling too frightening and prefer to walk holding a reassuring hand.

As children begin to control different aspects of their physical bodies, they play physically. For example, children might play by hopping along in the direction they want, at the speed they want, where they want, making their body do as they wish, controlling the situation. It is essential to the process of play that the child is in control.

Games have rules which are given in play. Children make their own rules

EMOTIONAL AND SOCIAL

Davies (1995, p. 114) says 'all movement is expressive'. For example, she says children:

> ▶ jump for joy
> ▶ shake with excitement
> ▶ inch forward cautiously
> ▶ hold back with reticence
> ▶ hit out in anger
> ▶ slump in dejection
> ▶ rise to the occasion
> ▶ dig in their heels
> ▶ throw themselves whole-heartedly into their play

Children are very rarely still when they play. They move about, and their movements show their feelings. In chapter 3 feelings are explored more deeply.

MORAL AND SPIRITUAL

One of the most important things about being a human being is being able to pretend. This means making one thing or person stand in place of another. Pretend play, as Dunn's work (1988) shows, helps children to do this. The child pretends to be the parent, for example. Pretend play allows children to experiment and try out different ideas, feelings and relationships with people. It also helps children to think of others, and care about them. It helps children to explore what it is like to be unkind and angry without upsetting anyone. Respecting other people is the foundation of moral and spiritual learning. The child pretending to be a parent is showing how his or her parent might feel when angry, or pleased with a child's behaviour.

Pretend play does not help children to explore just their own feelings, it also helps them to explore how other people feel. This is called decentring.

Summary

> ▶ Play becomes a resource to be used in later adult life.
> ▶ Play helps children to be more resilient in life.
> ▶ Play is a central part of human development.
> ▶ Play helps children in:
>   – physical learning
>   – emotional and social learning
>   – intellectual and spiritual learning

2

What is Play?

Play is part of a network of developmental and learning strategies

Children need to develop a variety of different developmental and learning strategies. Young children do not develop and learn only through their play, but play is one important way of developing and learning for them.

Play co-ordinates a network of learning strategies, linking them so that learning makes sense to the child.

The network of development and learning – which includes play

> ▶ Children and adults develop and learn through first-hand experiences.
> ▶ Children and adults develop and learn about their culture through taking part in games with rules.
> ▶ Children and adults develop and learn about keeping hold of their experiences by representing them in drawings, models, dances, drama, talking to each other and symbols of all kinds (for example, numbers).
> ▶ Children make sense of what they have learnt through their play. (See Figure 2.1.)

Recognising quality play

It can be very confusing to look at young children bustling about busily, and to wonder what it is all about. So often young children seem to be 'busy doing nothing', but things are not always as they seem in life.

The more researchers and people who work with young children make it a priority to observe what is going on, the more important the young child's 'busyness' seems to be.

FIRST-HAND EXPERIENCE
- First-hand experience is basic to active and interactive learning.
- Without real experiences a child's learning doesn't relate to life.
- Real experiences happen through being with people, and through actively using objects and materials.
- Young children have not lived as long as adults, and so they have not had as much experience which they can use to learn through. Their need for real experiences cannot be over-emphasised.

PLAY
- Play co-ordinates learning.
- It brings together the different kinds of learning in the network.
- Play brings about the deepest kind of learning.
- Play helps children to understand and make sense of what they have been learning through their ideas, feelings and relationships.
  - Play helps children to learn the things they know and understand, and to make connections.

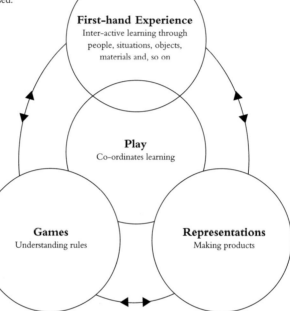

GAMES
- Games help children to understand rules that are made by someone else.
- Games help children to take part and fit into a culture.
- Different types of games include:
  - **social games** which consist of greetings, partings and customs between people from different cultures.
  - **performance games**, such as acting out the script of a play, performing a choreographed dance, performing a piece of composed music, which are different according to the culture they are from.
  - **mathematical games** including chess or word games such as scrabble, which introduce scientific and language rules.
  - **sports** – another kind of cultural game.
- Through games children learn how rules are made, how to keep rules and change rules in ways which are agreed between people.
- Children learn who has authority and must be obeyed. They learn how to conform (fit in). Games give a sense of belonging and being part of a community. Knowing the rules of the game means knowing some of the rules of the culture.
- Games make children feel secure.

REPRESENTATION
- Representation is a way of keeping hold of experiences. It means children create and make products which can be kept.
- Songs, dances and stories can be created and kept by writing them down. Then they can be performed again and again.
- Drawings, paintings and models can be created.
- Ideas can be kept by talking about them in words, or using sign language. They can be made into written creations. Numbers are another kind of written product.
- Children often use their creative products as play props, or turn them into games which can be repeated again and again.
- Children need to represent their own experiences, not those of other people. It is no good asking them to draw a bee if they have never looked closely at one. The drawing must be about **their** experience of a bee, or it will be only superficial learning.

Figure 2.1   The network of learning

It is useful to be able to suggest what kind of learning is going on, and to identify where it belongs in the network of learning.

When observing play ask yourself these questions:

> ► **Is the child learning through a first-hand experience?**
> The learning might be through a real experience of finding out what happens when a lump of clay is rolled in the hands of a three-year-old. The lump becomes a sausage shape.
>
> ► **Is the learning through a game?**
> The learning might be through a game – singing and dancing a ring game during group time, and using the rule that at the end of the line everybody claps their hands. For example, 'If you are happy and you know it, clap your hands' is a song that has this rule.
>
> ► **Is the learning through representation?**
> The learning might be through representation. Martin (four years) saw a fish being caught and saw its mouth opening and shutting, gasping for water. He found a box with a lid and opened and shut it to represent the fish. Later he showed it to his father and repeated it.
>
> ► **Is the learning through play?**
> Below are twelve ways to recognise whether quality play is present. If you can see seven or more of these twelve indicators, you are probably observing quality play.

The indicators for play

1. Children use the real first-hand experiences that they have in life.
2. Children make up rules as they go along when they play. 'I am a hungry cat, and when I say miaow, you feed me.'
3. Children often use their representations as play props in their play. For example, having made a biscuit out of clay, it is then used for playing the tea break in an office.
4. Children will choose to play. They cannot be made to play.
5. Children rehearse the future and role play. 'I am a shopkeeper selling things.'
6. Children pretend when they play, for example that a stone is a potato.
7. A child might play alone, for example with the dolls' house or garage.

Real gardening is an experience which might become a play theme

8. Children might play together.
   a) Children might play in **parallel**. For example both children put dolls to bed in the home area as companions together, but they do not take much notice of each other.
   b) Two children might play as a pair **associatively**. One might be the chef in the restaurant, while the other is the waitress, but they still might not have very much to do with each other.
   c) Two children might play as a pair **co-operatively**. One might be the baby, the other might be the nurse. The nurse might give medical treatment to the baby.
   d) A group of children might play together co-operatively. There will be at least one leader, several followers and perhaps others to negotiate the play. The leader will help everyone to keep the play flowing well so that it does not break down. Leaders arise quite naturally.
9. There will be a play agenda for each person playing. If adults join the play, their agenda is no more important than that of the children.
10. Children playing will be deeply involved. It will be difficult to distract them from their play, because play is deep learning. This is sometimes called **wallowing in play**.

Celebrating being able to hop during play

11. Children try out their recently acquired skills and competencies, for example hopping, which involves being able to go in the direction they want, at the speed they want, so they feel in control.
12. Children playing are co-ordinating the ideas and feelings they have, and making sense of them. They are sorting out the relationships they have with people and how their culture works.

PLAY INDICATOR ONE – CHILDREN USE FIRST-HAND EXPERIENCE IN THEIR PLAY

In playing offices, children might use their own experience of visiting an office, stamping letters, 'pretend' writing, answering the telephone, photocopying, making cups of tea and so on.

A group of children, all of whom had visited an office, decided to play at offices. A three-year-old boy knew how to use a photocopier. He played this by simply re-enacting this everyday event quite realistically.

His sister, who is one year old, does not understand about offices, but she does understand about having drinks, and she wanders into the play with the older children and pretends to drink out of a cup.

A four-year-old friend knew about answering the telephone and writing. He played out these activities, but they were a bit more elaborate than the play of his three-year-old friend. He was developing the everyday real events of an office and making himself into the character of somebody who works in an office. He was beginning to extend this into a little story or narrative about being an office worker.

As they become older and more used to playing, children begin to extend and elaborate on their real first-hand experiences (Fein, 1981).

A group of children, seven to nine years of age, also played offices, but they made an advance plan together. They worked out who they would be (characters) and a story or narrative (plot). They dressed up and made play props for the different characters. They came to pay bills, sign cheques, write to people, tele-phone them. They were the office for a dress shop that is called 'Lady Jane'. There was a complaints department, an orders department and a sales department. These were all based on their real experiences of shopping, offices and the Gas Board showroom (hence the complaints department).

The older children had more elaborate play scenes than the younger children who simply made use of the real everyday experiences.

PLAY INDICATOR TWO – CHILDREN MAKE UP RULES SO THAT THEY CAN KEEP CONTROL OF THEIR PLAY

A six-year-old boy, Mark, is taking part in a game of hopscotch. He is controlled by the rules of the game. Then he begins to pretend each square is a field. He throws the stone in the square and says it is a bird landing on the farmer's field, trying to eat the seeds.

He makes a rule with his friend, Simon, that if the stone lands on the field before Simon shouts 'Hey!', the bird has to leave. If not, the bird can stay and eat the seeds

The Opies (1988), who studied children's singing games and street games, found that children often begin with a game, such as hopscotch. Once they feel relaxed and start to trust each other, they begin to move into play. Instead of being controlled by the rules of the game, they can begin to take control and play together. But first, they have to trust each other enough to do this.

Piaget (1962) and Vygotsky (1978) thought that from about seven years old onwards children moved more and more into games rather than play. However, it may be that even children of this age need a game to start them off. Mark and Simon began with the security of a game of hopscotch, and then, when they sensed that they could manage it, they moved into play, which is more demanding and difficult.

Clody (three years) plays alone with her doll in the bath. She pushes the doll under the water, and laughs with glee every time the doll bobs to the surface and floats. This 'push and watch' play is completely controlled by her. The rules she makes during her play will fade when her bathtime finishes.

PLAY INDICATOR THREE — CHILDREN OFTEN USE THEIR REPRESENTATIONS AS PLAY PROPS WHEN THEY PLAY

Carly (five years) made a puppet out of a wooden peg. She wrapped a piece of blue material around the peg and tied it with string. She drew a face on the top part of the peg with a felt pen. She was representing Mary in the Christmas story. She then went to the dolls' house and made her the character of a mother, and played mummies and children, using the dolls in the dolls' house as babies and children. The peg doll became a play prop for her play.

PLAY INDICATOR FOUR — CHILDREN CHOOSE TO PLAY. OTHER PEOPLE CANNOT MAKE THEM PLAY

John (four years) saw his friends rush to the scrambling net and Joe shouted 'We are pirates! Climb the rigging!' He quickly joined them. The adult noticed that Meryl (three years) was watching. He asked if she would like to play pirates. Meryl said 'No'. The early childhood worker did not try to make Meryl play. Instead he stayed beside her and commented on the play. 'They are climbing the rigging now, aren't they? Joe is the look-out I think, isn't he? He is looking to see if they are near land, I think.'

He helped Meryl to see what play is about. Younger children often need to spend time watching play before they become willing to play. They really appreciate adults who help them to watch, and adults who help them to join in when they feel ready for play with other children. You can read about helping children to play with other children and finding access strategies to do this in chapter 3.

PLAY INDICATOR FIVE — CHILDREN REHEARSE ADULT LIFE IN THEIR PLAY

Children often take on an adult role-play, becoming post people, refuse collectors, bus conductors, parents, doctors and others. They drive cars, go shopping, make cakes and go to the bank. Role-play is one of the best ways to prepare for adult life.

> Sade (four years) played parking the car. She pretended to drive around with a pretend steering wheel, and tried to find parking spaces. She parked, looking behind her, and then put money in the parking meter. 'I am parking my car,' she told an adult.

As children become more experienced, they can add more and more to their role-play. Their play becomes more and more complex.

> Sue (four-and-a-half-years) joins Sade. 'Pretend I am the traffic warden and you are late, and I give you a ticket.'

These children can co-ordinate the roles they are playing. This means they can get more out of their play. Later on, they may write about these characters as they begin to write creative stories.

> Two-year-old Bobby knows how adults have drinks and sits with one leg crossed over the other, pretending to drink in a grown-up way. Bobby is imitating the way her mother moves and sits when drinking tea. This is the beginning of role-play. Bobby is rehearsing for adult life.

The children in Lady Jane dress shop are able to take on a wider range of adult roles, and can make all the characters interact with each other. Their role-play is getting very near to being a drama improvisation around a theme that they have all agreed in advance.

Let's pretend

PLAY INDICATOR SIX — CHILDREN PRETEND IN THEIR PLAY

Once children realise that one thing or one person can be made to stand for another, they can pretend play. 'Let's pretend' is probably one of the most important developments in a child's life.

> 'Pretend this cup is a bucket and this floor,' said five-year-old Frances. doll carries water in it to wash a

Judy Dunn (1988) found that even one-year-olds can pretend play with the help of brothers and sisters or parents. They pretend to be naughty and are willing to let a brother or sister pretend to tell them off when they play. In real life they would be very upset by this.

Pretending allows children to transform real life. Transforming means changing things from how they really are. They can try things out safely.

What would it be like to be naughty when Grandma comes to tea? What would it be like to go to hospital? What would it be like to live on the moon? What would it be like if my brother died? What would it be like to bully the baby? Children can explore all kinds of ideas, feelings and relationships when they pretend.

It is one thing for four-year-olds to pretend **how they might feel** when going to hospital. However an exciting development of pretend play occurs when children pretend **how someone else would feel**.

> 'She thinks it is going to hurt (the doll) so she cries. When she cries and the nurse tells her it won't hurt, darling. But pretend the child does not understand.'

In this situation four-year-old Sam is thinking himself into being a toddler who is going to hospital. Sam is trying to think how the toddler might react to hospital treatment. He keeps saying 'pretend' because he needs to make it clear, even to himself, that this is not real. This is play. This is play about what it is like to be a toddler going to hospital.

PLAY INDICATOR SEVEN – CHILDREN SOMETIMES PLAY ALONE

It used to be thought that it was more advanced for a child to play with others co-operatively than to play alone whether other children were available or not (Parten, 1933). However, it is really a question of mood and moment. There are times when children need and want to play alone, and times when they are best playing with other children.

> Tom (three years) is on the beach. He likes the pebbles and wipes them with wet seaweed, watching the water change the colour of the pebble as he does so. He puts the pebbles in a row. He picks them up and makes a new row. The pebbles are under his control as he plays with them, deeply involved and deeply alone. To disturb him now would be to damage his play.
>
> Anthea (six years) is playing with her dolls' house. She talks in different voices as the characters have conversations.

Alistair (four years) also talks out loud as he plays with his small world street scene. He is at a nursery school. The staff are careful to protect this type of deep and solitary play. He is not disturbed by other children who are encouraged to respect each other's solo play from an early age.

PLAY INDICATOR EIGHT – AT TIMES CHILDREN PLAY IN PAIRS OR GROUPS

a)   *Companionship play or parallel play*

Companions (Findlay, 1994) like to be together when they play, but they do not want to talk to each other. They do not take much notice of each other.

Alistair and Anthea, who both enjoy small world play, play side-by-side at two dolls' houses placed together on a table. Interestingly, they both, quite separately, put the furniture in rows. It is as if both are aware of what the other is doing, but that is enough. They do not need to communicate directly with each other.

b)   *Associative play*

Shanaz (three years) was in the garden in an early years setting. She went to the mud patch where a group of children were pretending to be digging up treasure. She joined in, but when Zak (four years) suggested 'Let's pretend we are digging up worms. We are fishing,' she carried on digging for gold. She enjoyed digging like the others, but she was playing a different theme from the other children.

c)   *Co-operative play in a pair and in a large group*

Siobhan and Amanda are beginning to find out about co-operative play. Siobhan (thirteen months) picked up a teddy. Amanda (fourteen months) immediately did the same. Siobhan dropped her teddy, Amanda did the same. Siobhan repeated this and so did Amanda. Siobhan shrieked with laughter. So did Amanda. They were playing co-operatively, making up the rules as they went along.

By the age of five years James and Caroline can spend an afternoon playing with Action Man and Sindy. They both have their own play ideas of course, but, in co-operative play, all the different ideas become involved. The children link and connect their play ideas. They decide that Action Man goes on an expedition and Sindy joins him. They dress her in his clothes because she can't wear high heels on a mountain.

Thinking things out – an advance script

With this kind of play, the children spend a lot of time thinking things out, and planning things in advance, because the theme becomes quite complicated.

It is a kind of advanced script that they make together. They decide what is going to happen. They negotiate the story and how the characters will behave, so that they do not have to consider this once they get deeply into the flow of play.

d)   A group of children playing together

> Gaia (seven years) and Hanja (five years) were spending the afternoon with Andy (seven years) and David (seven years). Gaia wanted to play hospitals, but the boys did not. She suggested the boys go off to war and that she and Hanja would be nurses in the army hospital.

The two separate themes would move along side-by-side, and everyone could have what they wanted in the play.

These children did not know each other very well, but this was a good way of getting together without needing the complete trusting of one another which is so vital for the deepest levels of co-operative play.

PLAY INDICATOR NINE – ADULTS CAN JOIN IN THE PLAY, OR START THE PLAY, BUT THEY MUST NOT TAKE OVER THE PLAY

If adults want to join the play, they need to do three things:

1. Observe the children and try to work out each child's personal play theme.

> All the children are playing shops. However, Joe, who is three years old, keeps pretending to put things in baskets. Raffat, five years old, keeps trying to give people change and says thank you to all his customers. Sandra, four years old, keeps going out and coming back into the shop.

These are the personal play themes that children have within the central theme of shopping.

2. Adults need to support the personal play themes of children. For example, the adult might become a shopkeeper and give Joe things to put in his basket when he shops. Another time the adult might become a customer and buy things from Raffat so that he can be the shopkeeper. Later, the adult might become someone who is on their way to the shops and stops for a chat with Sandra when she is on her way to a different shop.

   In other words, adults must see where they are needed in order to support the children's play themes. When they do this, adults also become role models and children see the advantages of taking different roles. It deepens their play, and keeps it flowing with quality.

3. Adults need to extend the play.

   Once adults have worked out how to help children in a supportive way, they can encourage children to elaborate their play themes. They might do this by talking to the children.

A group of three- to five-year-olds were playing jumble sales. The adult kept dressing up and coming back as all sorts of different characters. The children began to play in a much more elaborate way when the adult joined the play.

Adults can also encourage children by helping them to find the props that they need for their play. For example, the children might need a counter in the shop, or a box to make a good pretend cash register, or some buttons they can use as pretend money. It is always interesting to see which children need very realistic props and which need just a suggestion like the box or the buttons. Some children pretend and do not need props at all. They mime giving the money, as Raffat did. It may be that to get them going, children need quite realistic props, but once their play is flowing together, they can use less realistic props and imagine more. Play encourages the imagination.

Play indicator ten — in play children are deeply involved in ideas, feelings and relationships

This involvement is sometimes described as wallowing in play.

Play involves children in ideas

Carl (three years) pretends to be a hen in a cage. He has heard his parents discussing the eggs that they buy, and deciding to buy free range eggs. He uses a cardboard box. He calls his sister Emily (fourteen months) and asks her to climb in with him. 'Pretend we are hens in this cage.' He is playing out the idea of battery hens in cages.

Play involves children in feelings

Hayley (two years) was playing putting her baby doll to bed. She made the baby cry when she walked away. Then she said 'go to sleep' but made the baby go on crying. It was very realistic and her mother stopped washing up and went over to see her and asked if she was all right. Hayley ignored her mother and carried on with the play. She was so deeply involved in her play that she did not hear her mother.

Play involves children in relationships

Barbara (six years) and Katie (five years) play at being 'spoilt girl and her mother'.

Barbara has temper tantrums and her mother gives in to everything she wants. The children are exploring the relationship between parents and children, and what this involves.

Play indicator eleven — children show their skills and competencies and what they know and understand in their play

Leo (four years) and Jason (six years) made a den in the garden. They knew how to put sticks together and tie them in a teepee style. They knew they needed two blankets to cover this and how to join the blankets with safety pins. Jason could sew tapes on to the opening and Leo wanted to tie those to shut the door. They spent ages in the preparation of their play props, but not so much time actually playing. The play itself was mostly about going out and shooting animals for supper and then pretending to eat them in the den. There were pretend night times with constant attacks from wild animals to wake them up.

Unfortunately, just when children are beginning to elaborate the techniques and skills of their play, they often begin to attend formal school where play is not encouraged. Since many children go home and watch TV or play computer games, there is little opportunity for play.

PLAY INDICATOR TWELVE – PLAY CO-ORDINATES A CHILD'S DEVELOPMENT AND LEARNING

Play brings together and connects different parts of the network of learning. It uses real first-hand experiences, games with rules, representation, and helps children to reflect on and try out ideas, feelings and relationships. Play co-ordinates a child's development and learning.

Summary

> ▶ Play is an important part of the child's development and learning.
> ▶ Indicators for play
>   1. Play uses a child's first-hand experiences.
>   2. Children make up rules in order to keep control of their play.
>   3. Play encourages children to make play props or mime things or people.
>   4. Children cannot be made to play.
>   5. Children rehearse adult roles and life as they play.
>   6. Children pretend when they play and transform real life.
>   7. Children play alone.
>   8. Children might play together in pairs or groups.
>   9. Adults can play with children but must not take over their play.
>   10. Children at play can be deeply involved and concentrating hard.
>   11. Children show their skills and what they know in their play.
>   12. Play co-ordinates ideas, feelings and relationships and promotes development and learning.
> ▶ If seven or more of these play indicators are present, you are probably observing quality free-flow play.

3

How Adults Can Help Children Play

Adult approaches to play

Inspectors (OFSTED) are critical of two approaches to play used by adults working with young children.

1. Too little help – just occupying children
    When children are left to themselves and told to play, their play does not show progress. Children are often sent off to the sand tray, water tray, home area or the wooden block area and told to play. However, children need support and help in their play.
2. Too much help – too many adult-led tasks
    Sometimes children are overloaded with too much 'help, guidance and teaching' in their play. Children need to be encouraged to make choices, decisions, take risks, and try out their own ideas, feelings and relationships when they play.

It is a question of finding the right balance between not helping children enough and giving them too much help so that it damages their play.

Adults need to work as a team, deciding where to be in the indoor or outdoor areas so that all areas are covered.

Helping children to play

> ▶ **Help children to stay in the role or character they create.**
> If they quarrel about who will push the baby in the pram, find another pram so each can have one, or help them to resolve it.
> For example, the adult might say something like 'Janie, you push the pram because you are the Mummy. Midge, perhaps you can sit on the pram and be pushed along because you are the big sister.'
> ▶ **Help children to stay in their theme or story.** Help them to

keep the play theme flowing along, for example a shopping theme. Adults can make suggestions such as 'Are you going to the Post Office next? No? You are going to the market are you? I see. These boxes might make a good market stall for you to use.'

The strategies used in the above examples in helping children to develop a role, or develop a play theme are:

a) finding the same equipment (for example, two prams)
b) helping children to negotiate with each other
c) suggesting but not forcing an idea (the boxes might be turned into a market stall)

Knowing the children well is essential so that more intervention is made with less able or less well-adjusted children.

▶ **Give the youngest children (0–3 years) everyday experiences, such as meals, sleeping or shopping.** This will provide children with the basics they need in order to play. The more children participate in everyday routines the more they can use these in their first efforts at pretend play. When children first begin to pretend play, they will pretend to eat or go to sleep or go to the shops.

▶ **Encourage creative activities.** Telling stories, dancing and singing songs with children, making models, drawings and paintings will provide them with stories and ideas to use in their play. These activities will feed into play themes, roles and play props and help play to develop.

▶ **Develop your skills in observation and assessment.** Adults who are good observers are in a position to both support and extend children in their play. Whether you work as part of a team or alone, you must assess the quality of play, and also consider your own skills for promoting play.

▶ **Help with access strategies.** Some children do not know how to join the play. Adults can show children that a side-by-side strategy is often a good one. 'Do you want to be a farmer too and dig in the field? There is a spade. Just pick that up and go and dig with the others, but I don't think I would ask whether you could join them. I would just go and dig if I were you.'

Children who ask to join the play are usually told 'No!' and rejected. Vivian Gussin Paley (1994) emphasises how important it is that a child should not feel rejected from group play.

▶ **Help children to be sensitive to each other.** This is a fundamental part of learning to play. It helps children to become caring about other people and to think how it feels to be someone else. For example, Joe (five years) says 'Let's play new boys and girls. I am new and you won't let me play. You say go away.'

Adults who encourage children to be different characters (roles), as Joe is doing, help children with their social, moral and spiritual development.

▶ **Protect children in their play.** The child who has spent an hour building a beautiful multi-storey car park with the wooden blocks needs to feel able to leave it while she goes to fetch the toy cars. Then she can use her representation of the car park as a play prop and begin to play multi-storey car parks with all the people who use it as characters in her play.

Children sometimes ask adults to watch a model for them, while they leave it for a moment. Adults need to offer help too. This encourages the kind of atmosphere in which play flourishes. Knowing an adult is there to help when it matters gives children a feeling of power and deepens their play.

▶ **Ensure there is enough equipment for the number of children.** Large enough lumps of clay or dough with large enough sand-pits and water trays are not difficult or expensive to provide. If there are not enough small world dolls, for example, they can be made out of pipe cleaners. Sand or water can be put in buckets and washing-up bowls.

Children love to be involved and quickly begin to make their own play props. It helps children to realise that equipment does not have to be fought over and that if there is not enough, something can be done about it. It also helps children to understand that not all equipment comes ready-made or bought. It can be made out of bits and bobs and found materials.

▶ **Make arrangements for sharing limited equipment.** If there is only one set of wooden blocks, then it has to be decided whether all the children can play with them at the same time or how turns should be taken.

Children usually learn about being fair in this way, providing adults help them. Discussing with children what might be a solution to the problem will actually help them more in the long term than if the adult makes a rule that only four children can play with the wooden blocks. Of course it makes more work for the adult, but it is more satisfying because by the time children reach middle childhood (8–12 years), they are much better able to negotiate and find solutions to problems by themselves.

Summary

- ▶ Low quality play occurs if:
  - children are left to themselves to play
  - adults control the play
- ▶ Play will be of deep quality if adults find effective ways of helping children to play so that they:
  - keep their character or role
  - keep their theme or story
  - have the materials and equipment they need
  - are helped to negotiate
  - are given suggestions but are not made to take them up
  - are helped with everyday play at first (for example, mealtime play)
  - are helped to elaborate their play schemes as they become more experienced (for example, going to the moon)
  - are shown the possibilities for pretending
  - talk together about play ideas
  - help children through access strategies to join and play in a group
  - are helped to think about what it is like to be someone else
  - are protected from children who might intentionally or unintentionally damage their play
  - have enough equipment
  - arrange to share limited equipment
- ▶ Adults need to keep regular records of their observations and assessments of children playing (Harding and Meldon-Smith, 1996; Bartholomew and Bruce, 1993).

4

Adults Giving Children Special Help in Their Play

In this chapter, four areas are considered:

> ▶ the sick child
> ▶ children with special educational needs
> ▶ child protection
> ▶ therapy

The sick child

Children who are sick are challenged in their play. They need a great deal of support and help, especially if they are confined to bed or convalescing. Small world and doll play can be very successful.

> Mannie (seven years) was in bed for several weeks, unable to move about very much. Her mother brought her a box of dolls from several countries which she had collected when she was a child. They decided where these dolls would live on the bed. For example, the Swiss doll was put on top of Mannie's legs (on a mountain) and the Dutch doll was put on the flat area at her feet (as Holland is a low, flat country).

Because she could not move much, her mother helped her to play by walking the dolls about, for example to visit each other. When her mother had to go to answer the telephone, Mannie spoke the voices of the dolls and pretended they were moving about. At seven years old this was possible for her to do in her play.

Another possibility is to have roads linking villages or towns. Little cars can move between, and string or ribbon can mark out the roads. Roads can go over mountains or hills and cars can carry post or parcels, or supplies to a

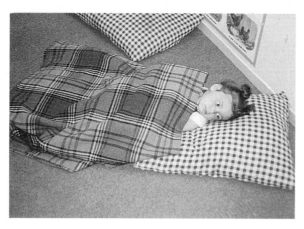

Waiting while a friend goes to find 'play people' to put by the bed

factory or shop, or all sorts of possibilities. The child's body can be the mountain.

For children in bed, play often begins by the adult telling a story (for example, Postman Pat) or making up a story and using the props to show the child the possibilities. If the props are left in an attractive box or basket near at hand, the child might begin to spontaneously play with some of these ideas.

Jan was four years old and played the card game 'Happy Families' with one of the nurses in hospital. She had been playing with cards using the village idea in the way described in the last example. She began to use the cards as people in the villages and put different people to live in different places. She concentrated for nearly an hour, using different voices for the different characters. The cards gave her a baker, grocer, butcher and others for her play scenario.

Felt boards are useful for a child in bed to make play scenarios. A cheaper way of helping children to play than a felt board is to use a large piece of card covered in towelling, and scraps of paper, materials, twigs, leaves, string and similar materials which can give the child play props that can become all sorts of play situations. A whole picture can be created and made to come alive in this way. The adult might need to show the possibilities before the child (usually four years old or more) begins to play by him- or herself after a while.

Dorothy (four years) made a pile of wood to burn. She had little twigs and pretended she was making a bonfire. She played bonfires for half an hour or so using her card and scraps of material.

Paper dolls with paper clothes to fit over are good for play in bed. These can be made or bought. John (six years) played 'old-fashioned times' when he dressed dolls in Victorian costumes. He had a book about a Victorian house and opened the pages and pretended the dolls lived in the different rooms.

Dolls' houses (not too high so that the child in bed can reach the upper floors) and toy garages and cars can be placed on the bed table. A ball of string or masking tape can be used to make roads or gardens on the table.

It is very difficult for the youngest children to play in bed, as so much of their time is normally spent transporting things, putting things in and out of containers, bashing, pushing and pulling. However, some of this play can be provided for in bed. A box with a lid full of bits and bobs can be placed on the bed table. Two or three more boxes can be put around the child on the bed.

Young children seem to automatically start putting things in and out of containers given half a chance. They often become very involved in this kind of simple play.

A child from toddler age on who is sick may appreciate being able to paint or enjoy finger painting. Plastic sheets can be put over the bed, and the bed table can have a large tray with pots of paint on it. Brushes should not be too tall, or they get in the way and over-balance. There can be a variety of thick and thin brushes. Children like to have variety and choice in the brushes they use. A tray of thick paint for finger painting can also be placed on the bed table. Play dough or clay can be provided, as long as there are plastic covers on the bed and over the child.

There are some recipes for cookery that do not need cooking in an oven or on a stove, for example, biscuit cake or a winter salad. Again, plastic covers on the bed make this practical. If it is important that children do not eat clay, dough, things they have cooked or sweet things, then this will not be appropriate. If they are on any kind of diet it might be more appropriate to have a pretend tea party with dolls sitting on the bed eating pretend paper sandwiches, for example. Children enjoy drawing food and cutting it out to use in doll play.

When the paint play, clay, dough or cookery is finished, a large jug of water and a towel can quickly clean the child, who may want to spend some time on water play! Having a large bowl with not too much water in it means that spillages are less frequent. There needs to be enough water for play, though. A large bowl of clean water can have little boats floating on it and cups or other containers for pouring. If, because of their condition, children cannot get their hands, arms or faces wet, then this kind of play is not appropriate.

Children are helped to prepare themselves for hospitalisation or out patient visits by adults encouraging them to act out stories about going to hospital. There are story books which can be used, but acting out stories with small dolls or realistic props (syringes, stethoscopes, for example) gives children an idea of what is to come. The adult can pretend to give the doll an injection and say 'This might hurt a bit, but it won't hurt for long. When I take the needle out the pain will go.'

Children react much more positively in hospital settings if they are well prepared, and given honest information about what will happen to them and what will hurt or be uncomfortable. Children might later pretend play their real hospital experiences, especially if the props are left nearby for them to use.

Children with special educational needs

Children who have a physical or a learning disability need special help if they are to play. For children with learning disabilities, it is often the pretend aspects of play which are the most challenging. This is because pretending means the child needs to understand that one person or thing can stand for another. Once children understand this, they can transform reality. Play opens up a whole new way of thinking that frees children from the constraints of everyday life.

For children who are just beginning to understand that one thing can stand for another, it is important to make symbols very close to real life. For example, pretending to drink from a real cup, or eat from a real plate.

It used to be thought that children with multiple disabilities could not play, but in recent years this view has changed. Being able to play is now seen as every child's right, and is included in the International Charter of Children's Rights.

Babies and toddlers also need pretend situations which are based on everyday life situations which are very familiar to them. It is usually children from four years of age who manage pretend ideas such as going to the moon or living under the sea.

Children with disabilities will find these play themes more demanding, and some may not manage such far removed ideas. Children will need real experiences in order to reach the point where they can pretend play. For example, if children are introduced to fish swimming about in an aquarium, they are more likely to move into these play themes like most other children.

One of the reasons why children with disabilities have been held back in their play is that in the past it was not thought important to give them the same broadening experiences as most children. Alice Honig (1985) calls this a **double delay** in their progress. She says that first the children are disabled. Then they are deprived of enriching experiences which are part of most children's lives.

In chapter 1, it was emphasised that children need to move about freely and experience life fully through their senses. When this is not possible or easy, for example for a child who is profoundly deaf or visually impaired, or has a severe learning disability, or is a wheelchair user, adults need to work hard to enable them to have the experiences which most children can take for granted. It may take much more effort on everyone's part, but it could mean providing access for a child to play (Neilsen 1992).

Giving children their right to play is a great reward for adults working with children with physical or learning disabilities.

Children need freedom of movement

Child protection

In their play, children sometimes reveal aspects of their lives which signal to adults that there are issues requiring child protection. Children who are physically, sexually, emotionally or intellectually abused may well say or do things in their play which they would not be able to bring out in any other way.

It is important that adults respect what the child is 'saying' and are warm and supportive. It is also of great necessity that this play is immediately reported to the line manager, and monitored and recorded if the child is attending any kind of early years group. Confidentiality is essential.

The legal situation and the Children Act (1989) does not allow for the protection of children who are intellectually abused or intellectually neglected. However, if a child is thought to be physically, sexually or emotionally abused or neglected, the matter will be taken up by the Social Services Department (Bruce and Meggitt 1996).

Therapy

Helping children through play therapy requires specialist training. Neither nursery nurses nor early years teachers are trained as therapists. It is therefore important that children who have experienced emotional and physical pain are helped by trained experts. However, it is true to say that a child's play at home or in a group setting automatically encourages mental health. Adults who encourage children to play in the normal day-to-day situation are encouraging children to be resilient in their lives (see chapter 1).

When children have difficulties and challenges which block their play, therapy of one kind or another may be recommended.

The psychoanalytic approach

Although psychoanalytic therapists agree that play helps children in therapy, there is disagreement about the way that play can be used.

Melanie Klein worked in the 1920s and 1930s. She believed that when children play they show their innermost feelings and that they do this in ways which are deeply symbolic. Melanie Klein used to observe children when they were playing and then she would put into words what she thought were the symbolic messages of their play.

It was her belief that children had enough insight to be able to recognise the connection between what she said and the symbols of their play. She thought that as children began to understand themselves better in this way they would be able to adapt and find new ways of living their lives.

Anna Freud worked in the 1930s, 1940s and 1950s. She strongly disagreed with Melanie Klein's ideas about how to help children through play therapy. She thought that Melanie Klein was wrong to attempt interpreting children's play. She felt that the whole point about play was that it does not have deeper purposes which are symbolic. She used play as a means of diagnosing a child's problems. She used her observations of children playing to gather information about the child alongside interviews with parents. She felt that observing a child at play helped adults to see clearly the child's psychological state.

Non-directive therapy

This approach to therapy emerged through the work of people such as Carl Rogers in the 1940s and Virginia Axline in the 1960s. In this approach children are helped to become more self-aware and able to self-direct. They are encouraged to identify issues to express their feelings and to accept their own feelings. The emphasis is on creating a situation where a child feels totally accepted, free from criticism, and able to communicate.

The child is respected and allowed to use materials in the room as he or she wishes.

> ▶ The therapist tries to make a warm, friendly relationship with the child, even if it is difficult.
> ▶ The therapist is accepting of what the child does and says.
> ▶ The therapist establishes an atmosphere that gives permission to be oneself without probing questions or invitations to join particular kinds of play.
> ▶ The therapist reflects the child's feelings back to the child, but must not interpret too much.
> ▶ The therapist lets the child lead, and never hurries the child.

Some limits and boundaries are set in this approach because a child is limited in time, not allowed to damage materials, him- or herself or the therapist.

Structured approaches to play therapy

More recently therapists have begun to use a variety of structured approaches in which the therapist identifies the problem and then uses relevant play materials or activities in order to deal with it. This might involve using costume drama and dressing-up clothes, storytelling or art therapy.

Summary

> ▶ **Sick children**   Children who are sick can play even though the situation presents challenges. They need supportive adults, committed to finding ways to help them play, however difficult it might be.
> ▶ **Children with special education needs**   Children with special educational needs may also be constrained in their play. For some, there may be the challenge of using symbols to make one thing stand for another. Creating access to play for a child with a physical or learning disability means giving that child his or her rights, according to the International Charter of Children's Rights.
> ▶ **Child protection**   Sometimes in their play children reveal that there are serious issues of child protection taking place in their lives. These need to be reported to the line manager in strict confidence and recorded.
> ▶ **Play therapy**   Early childhood workers do not have the specialist training required to help children through play therapy. Different approaches are used by professional therapists to identify and deal with the problem.

5

Theories on Childhood Play

When people lived in caves, it is quite likely that their children played. However, adults did not begin to actively study childhood play until a few hundred years ago, and then mainly in Western cultures.

Separating work and play

> ▶ Early theories about play suggested that children need to relax and have more recreational time in between work times. Play is seen as a break from work.
> ▶ Another early theory proposed that children need to let off steam from the pressure that work builds up inside them.

These ideas separating work and play were popular in the last century but are no longer thought to be accurate.

Preparing for adult life

Gradually, from the 1920s, people thinking about childhood play began to see it as helping children to learn rather than as a break from learning.

One popular theory has been that play helps children to practise and prepare for adult life in a natural way (Groos, 1922; Bruner, 1990).

Play helps social and emotional development and learning

In the 1920s Sigmund Freud's theory of psychoanalysis had a great influence and helped early childhood workers to look at the emotional aspects of childhood play. Play helped children to move in and out of reality. It helped children to master and control their feelings. Then they could cope with their anxieties and conflicts. Play helps children to make sense of their experiences and to deal with their lives.

Anna Freud was the daughter of Sigmund Freud. Her work showed how play can help children who have experienced trauma to regain a sense of control over their lives. During the 1950s, she worked with children who had survived concentration camps in Hitler's Nazi Germany.

Her student, Erik Erikson, had a great influence from the 1950s. He helped adults to understand that play is important for not only a child's emotional well-being. Childhood play also has a long-term impact on the possibility for creativity in adults (artists, scientists and others).

Donald Winnicott in the 1950s showed how important something like a teddy bear can be for a child. He called such items 'transitional objects'. They help children to be with people they love, or away from them. They also help children to begin to play, because their teddy becomes a character to make play stories with.

Play helps intellectual/cognitive development and learning

From the 1920s, as it was gradually realised that emotional and social development are helped by play, those interested in young children began to understand that play also helps children to think. Thinking is about the intellectual (cognitive) aspects of development and learning.

From the 1920s Jean Piaget developed his theory that play helped children to assimilate, take in and make sense of experiences. He also thought it helped them to move more and more deeply into what he called 'symbolic behaviour' (pretend play) from the time they were toddlers. He was interested in the way children make one thing or a person stand for something else when they pretend. He thought that part of a child's learning was about adjusting to new ideas and that play was very important because it helped children to use the things that they know. He believed that play is mostly about using what you know.

Jerome Bruner's first ideas became influential in the UK during the 1960s, adding to Piaget's theories of play. Although Bruner uses the word 'play', he really emphasises the importance of games with rules. For instance, he looks at the game of peek-a-boo that babies and toddlers enjoy so much. He is interested in how games introduce children to their culture and prepare them for adult life.

Lev Vygotsky's ideas about play were not translated from Russian into English until 1978. They have had a great influence during the 1990s in the UK. He thought play showed children using their highest levels of learning. Vygotsky thought that play helped children to move from where they are in their thinking to a higher level. He said play allows children to move from their actual stage of development to a higher zone, which he called the 'zone of potential development'. He thought play was an important way in which children reach their zone of potential development.

There is one important difference between theories which emphasise feelings and theories which emphasise thinking and ideas. This is shown in the following chart.

Theories Emphasising Play, Feelings and Relationships	Theories Emphasising Play, Thinking and Ideas
	Play is important during childhood.
Play is seen as important during childhood. Play becomes a resource that can be used during adulthood for being creative as an adult.	As middle childhood approaches from about eight years of age, play turns into games with rules (for example, chess, tennis, football).
There is continuity between childhood play and adult creativity.	Play fades as children outgrow it. It is only important during early childhood.

Pioneers of childhood play in the UK

Through the influence of Froebel (1782–1852), McMillan (1860–1931) and Isaacs (1885–1948), play became an important part of a child's education in the UK. Froebel's pioneer work spread far beyond Germany where he lived: it became the main influence in the UK. Both Margaret McMillan and Susan Isaacs developed his work. By the 1960s the McMillan training colleges, the Froebel Educational Institute and the Child Development

Department at the Institute of Education in the University of London all trained teachers to encourage children to play in ways which helped their learning.

It was not until the period in which Susan Isaacs worked that psychological theories about play developed, and research evidence began to support the theories which suggested that play has a central place in the network for learning.

Summary

▶ Play is no longer seen to be about relaxing or letting off steam. That is called recreation.
▶ Play helps children develop and learn:
  – Early **pioneers for play** in the UK education system were Froebel, McMillan and Isaacs
  – **Social and emotional theories:** Sigmund and Anna Freud, Erikson, Winnicott. There is continuity between childhood play and adult creativity
  – **Intellectual/cognitive theories:** Piaget, Bruner, Vygotsky. Early childhood play fades to become games with rules which help children to take part in society

Creating Places to Play and Props for Play

Children are adventurers. They seize opportunities and find places to play wherever they can. The places to play in this chapter are chosen because they are examples of common situations where play can occur.

In the home

Judy Dunn's observations (1988) show that through play with their brothers, sisters or parents, children as young as a year old can be involved at a deep level in the kind of pretend play explored in chapter 2.

There are some traditional places to play in the home. These include under tables, behind sofas and chairs, putting sheets and blankets over tables, in cupboards, boxes, on mats or rugs. For example, in a home setting, a wardrobe had been moved from upstairs to downstairs and was waiting in the hallway to be taken in a van to a friend's house. It was stable and the doors were easy to open and shut. What could be a better place to play than an empty cupboard? It was soon made into a lift in a department store. At other times it was Dr Who's Tardis, a time machine. It could beam people up, as in *Star Trek*. It is important to say that an adult was always present when children played with the wardrobe. Ensuring that children are safe while they play is essential at all times.

In chapter 3 it was stressed that a young child's play does not just happen. Children are born with the potential for play, and they need to be helped if they are to find out how to play in any depth.

In different parts of the world, in different cultures, in different families, in different situations, in towns or rural areas or as travellers moving from place to place, in homes, schools or different kinds of group settings, children can be helped to play. Children need people who help them to play, and they need places to play:

> ▶ Children need places to play which are safe.
> ▶ Children need places which encourage them to play.
> ▶ Children need places which allow them freedom to develop their play.

Play develops best when adults actively create places which are good for play.

This means that it is important that adults are interested and on hand, and are skilled in knowing when to help, when to move in and when to hold back.

In this way children can get the most out of the places they decide to play in, perhaps building a den under the table, or in the garden. It is very important that adults create places for children to play both indoors and outdoors. This is because for many children in modern life, it is very difficult for them to play safely in the streets or parks.

Places which are underneath

Rather than endure or ban children from playing under a coffee table with a plant on it, which is not ideal, it might be worth finding a different table which children are allowed to play underneath. Another solution would be to move the plant! Given a bit of thought, tables can be perfect, safe places to play under in the home or in various kinds of group settings.

By putting a sheet or blanket over a table, walls are easily made. If there is not a carpet underneath, but lino or a wooden floor, the play can be made cosier by putting a rug under the table. Furniture can be made by collecting spare cardboard boxes from a shop. For example, one might be used as a table in a house.

Cushions make seats or beds. A box on its side can become a cupboard, with the flaps as cupboard doors. Crockery can be made from old yoghurt or margarine cartons.

If it is not practical or appropriate to turn a table into a den, often very large cardboard boxes are available from shops. Shopkeepers will be happy to have them collected at the end of the day and take pleasure in thinking that the box will be put to good use. The type that have had washing machines or tumble dryers in them are ideal.

Using found materials to enhance small world play

There are some very important signals that adults will be giving children when they provide these kinds of simple places to play in. Children will learn

> ▶ that everyday objects like a table or a large cardboard box can be put to different uses
> ▶ that adults try to support their play, and make a great effort to do this
> ▶ that play is happier without expensive toys
> ▶ that adults value play

However, it is important to remember that in some cultures, such as the Maori culture in New Zealand, children are taught that objects have a particular function. A table is something to be eaten from and not to be used in other ways. It might be appropriate for children to use a cardboard box for a den, rather than a table.

Inevitably, at home, there will come the time when a meal needs to be served on the table! It might be appropriate or fun to eat under the table. However, some meals or situations do not lend themselves to this. Then the cloth or blanket over the table can be removed, the furniture can be dragged out on the rug which was put under the table. The meal can be eaten in the normal way and after it is finished the play place can be easily reconstructed by dragging the rug with cardboard furniture on it back under the table.

In one home, the table had a shelf under it which was where an extra leaf could be put in the middle. Children playing under this table loved to keep stores there. But adults needed to check that heavy tins from the kitchen table did not fall on children's heads. Children were encouraged to think about safety aspects and store cereal boxes or lighter things on the shelf.

When children are helped to think about safety, they usually take responsibility for themselves more easily. They begin to care about other children, especially those younger than themselves.

Rearranging furniture behind chairs and making corners

Children sometimes rearrange furniture, or are helped to do so by adults, so that play places are made. For example, a folding foam bed can be made into a tent shape or a corner. These are very good for bouncing on or sliding down, as they cannot be damaged as easily as ordinary beds.

Chairs can also be made into walls and, with blankets or sheets over them, they can be very rewarding dens to play in.

Covering places over

Sometimes children like to cover the play places they make with a roof. Obviously it is dangerous to do so with anything heavy. Sheets, blankets and pieces of cardboard made from opening out large cardboard boxes are ideal. String makes it possible to tie the sheet on to the legs of furniture. Masking tape helps to make hinges and to join the cardboard pieces together. Children should not be left to use string or masking tape unsupervised.

It can be very frustrating for older children who enjoy making their dens more and more elaborate if the string slips down the pole. This is a good time to introduce the idea of a teepee. The forked top of the roof means that the string cannot slip down. Children from about four or five years of age can tie a bow. From about six or seven years of age they can be taught:

> ▶ a reef knot (not a granny knot which is too tight and impossible to undo)
> ▶ a bowline knot (as used in tying up boats and easy to undo)

Sometimes children might cover wide spaces on the floor. For example, Kate (four years) covered the whole floor from the front door to the kitchen and living room with pieces of newspaper. It looked like a huge mosaic. It took up a large part of the morning for her to do this. She said it was a field. She had recently spent a holiday in the countryside and seen fields looking like a patchwork.

Children often cover floors with blankets and patchwork of all kinds. They often create play scenarios with these and use small world animals and cars and people to make streets, farms, railways and other places in their play. Adults who respect children's needs to spread over a floor in the home or the group setting are helping children to create a successful place to play.

Sometimes children or adults like to define a space on the floor. Perhaps the play needs to stay on the mat because the children are pretending to be on a boat, in a spaceship, airplane or car. Staying on the mat becomes important. Getting off the mat might mean being eaten by a shark, or falling through the air. It might mean that the adult asks the children to stay in a particular area so that the wooden blocks do not spread all over the room.

Inside cupboards, under the stairs

Children are inclined to seek out cupboards which have possibilities as dens. This can be dangerous. There have been tragic cases of children climbing inside chest-type deep freezers, or accidentally being shut into airtight cupboards. One family made a safe den in a cupboard under the stairs. When the children grew up and left home, no-one could bear to dismantle it. It had a torch lantern, hanging on a hook, wall hangings made from favourite scarves, a box of books, pillows to curl up on.

Visiting children loved to play there, and, over the years, grandchildren began to use it for their play place. By the age of seven years or so, they would write messages to each other, leaving them for the next users of the cupboard. By nine or ten years of age they began writing in secret codes (giving the key to decipher messages).

On various occasions the cupboard had been a submarine, an airplane, a Tibetan underground house, a badger's house, a secret hideout for escaped soldiers and Robin Hood's hidden den in Sherwood Forest. It had memories and play moments lurking in it which were deeply important for all the children and adults who had played in it.

In the garden

In the garden there are often bushes, or perhaps a tree (for example a weeping willow) which create natural rooms. This kind of play place is easy to create because it is already there, made by nature. Where this is not possible, a clothes horse, sheets and large cardboard boxes can be used to make dens.

At the beach

Some beaches with large rocks and rockpools lend themselves in this way, with cave-like rooms and nooks and crannies which children will turn into play places. They might become bands of mountain brigands, King Arthur, explorers in space, jungles, rainforests or deserts.

As children develop their play, the themes they explore and the scenarios they create become more complicated and sophisticated. This tends to be from four years old. Many children stop being encouraged to play before they are five years of age in a variety of cultures. This means that their play fades and withers away before they develop rich, elaborate themes. Children deprived of the next level after everyday themes have been explored, such as playing mealtimes, do not know about the full possibility of play.

In an early years group setting

Until this point in the chapter, the emphasis has been on helping children to play in the home. When helping children to play in a larger group setting, the following ideas can be added.

Setting up a home area

The home area is probably one of the most important areas in an early childhood setting.

THE KITCHEN

A home area needs to reflect familiar aspects of the child's home. This means that it should have crockery, cutlery and cooking utensils in the western

European style, but also from other cultures. For example, Chinese cookery requires chopsticks, bowls and woks. These need to be available all the time so that children learn to use the appropriate utensils for different sorts of food preparation.

For children who may not know about woks, it will be important to include activities which introduce them to their purpose and function. In this way, children not only see their own culture reflected, but also have the opportunity to learn about other cultures in ways which hold meaning for them, and therefore are not tokenist. It is particularly important to introduce children to different cultures through the activities of daily life, such as cooking, because they can most easily relate to these events.

It is sometimes thought that children who do not meet other children from Afro-Caribbean, Asian, Chinese or traveller backgrounds have no need of these experiences. Nothing could be further from the truth. It is when children are ignorant about other cultures that overt or unwitting discrimination arises. Ignorance is a major cause of discrimination and of stereotyping people.

It is important that everything in the home area has a proper place, and that children are taught how to put things away. A large dresser with hooks for cups, and ample cupboards for saucepans and casserole dishes is a popular choice of equipment. Sets of things should not be mixed up, as this confuses everyone, and makes it difficult for the children to value the area and take a pride in keeping it looking attractive. There is also a great deal of mathematical learning in sorting out chopsticks from spoons, knives and forks, and Chinese soup spoons, or knowing which sets relate, for example, to Chinese life, which to Indian, or African cooking, and which to Europe.

> ▶ Ordering – which are biggest? which smallest?
> ▶ Matching and classifying – which things are the same?
> ▶ Sorting and seriating – which things are different and in which way?
> ▶ One-to-one correspondences – a cup for each person.

These questions are important in building up a child's understanding of number, patterns, sizes and shapes in mathematics.

It is important to consider safety in the home area kitchen. Plastic knives and forks are sometimes necessary if particular children are challenging in their behaviour but, on the whole, children of three to four years and upwards can take responsibility and use cutlery and chopsticks appropriately, providing their correct use is stressed and understood by the child. Decisions of this kind will need to be taken by the whole team of early childhood workers, who know the particular children with whom they are working.

On the other hand, glass or cooking knives are always a danger. Young children do not know enough about the scientific properties of materials like glass, and so plastic substitutes are needed. Picnic sets are useful in this respect.

It is also advisable to have plastic, unbreakable crockery, because of the expense of replacing brittle china sets, and the possibility of a child being cut. Children from four years old usually know enough about china crockery to take responsibility for its care. The type used by catering firms is the most suitable and hard-wearing.

Children with special educational needs may be using the home area, and they may need to have special arrangements in the kitchen area. A child in a wheelchair will need a lower table so that, for example, a mixing bowl can be stirred. It might be necessary to make a cooker of an appropriate height. This can be made from a cardboard box.

In relation to home-made equipment, it is important to include items made by adults for the children. Cookers, fridges and washing machines can be great fun to make with the children from cardboard boxes, and can be replaced regularly as they become shabby. This kind of play prop encourages children to think technologically, have ideas about designing and learn how to make things.

Commercially made equipment also has a place, although as discussed in chapter 7, it is important not to pre-structure too much. This stops children from moving into pretend, and keeps them wanting everything to be realistic. One of the most important things about a home area is that it has the possibility to move children out of the real world into imaginative and symbolic worlds. Commercial cookers and other equipment needs to be carefully chosen, so that it is strong enough to last for years. Natural wood lasts longer than painted wood, which soon chips and looks shabby, or plastic which splits or bends with constant use.

The important thing to remember is that children need equipment in the

home area which suggests and encourages the imagination and helps them to
have play ideas, feelings, and to play alone or with others.

The food the children cook will be of these kinds:

▶ pretend
▶ pre-structured (e.g. plastic fruit)
▶ transformable (e.g. dough)
▶ real food (ingredients for a winter salad)

It is important to remember that it is quite hard for a young child to simply
imagine food. Some three- to four-year-olds do, but usually it is the five- to
seven-year-olds who most easily manage this.

The trouble with pre-structured food, like plastic fruit, is that it tends to
keep children in the here and now. If there is a plastic apple, it tends to
produce a play about apples.

The advantage of transformable food is that the children bring their own
ideas to it. For example, dough can be made into roti, pancakes, pasties or
pies. It is best when dough is left in its natural colour and not coloured.
Dough, ideally made with the children helping, is an example of adults
presenting transformable food. Sometimes the children will make their own
transformable food. They might decide that a daisy is a fried egg, a leaf is a
plate, and a twig is a knife and fork, or a mud pie is mashed potato or rice.

Real food is often offered as a way for children to recreate a real cooking
experience. It may not encourage imaginative play. It is more likely to
encourage real cooking. It might not be wise to provide it in the home area
all the time. Many early childhood settings have a cooking area as part of
the basic provision in a different area of the room. This will be a different
kind of learning to the learning through play which is the focus of this
book.

THE LIVING ROOM

The living room might have a television, radio or CD player. Again, it is
important not to make it so real that it is simply a place to relive real life
situations. If children want to listen to real CDs or tapes, it might be more
useful and appropriate to create a listening area somewhere else, away from
the home area.

In a play place, the aim is to help children to pretend. This means that they make one thing stand for another. They transform real objects into something else in their mind. For example, a cardboard box makes a good television and children might be encouraged to act out television programmes a bit like a puppet show.

A series of wooden boxes makes an excellent investment because it will last almost forever. They can be transformed into tables and beds. Having books, newspapers, writing pads and pencils near a telephone helps children to learn about writing and reading. It is important to have any examples of writing in different languages and different kinds of scripts, such as English and also Urdu or Chinese. It is also important to encourage children to make their own props, for example folding large pieces of paper and doing pretend writing and drawing pictures to make a newspaper. These kinds of play prop will then be developed by children if adults show them the possibilities.

Often it is best not to teach children directly when it comes to play props. Storytime is an excellent way of showing children the possibilities for play props. For example, the adult might make a newspaper during the storytelling session and then put it in the home area. Children are very likely to play at reading newspapers after this. Also they are very likely to make their own newspapers and play with them in the home area.

Children gather ideas for play wherever they go. Creative children who know how to play are likely to become resourceful adults.

THE BEDROOM

Different beds create a wealth of mathematical experiences for children as they play. In real life, mathematics meets us at every moment. We cannot live without patterns, shapes, comparisons and contrasts and ways of ordering things in time, space and numbers. Mathematical thinking helps people to make sense out of experience and to organise it. It is therefore useful to have three beds: largest, middle-sized and smallest. Then there can be three sets of bedclothes, one to fit each bed.

There can be sets of dolls of different ethnic groups to fit on the differently sized beds, with different sets of dolls' clothes which are biggest, middle-sized and smallest. It is very important not to say 'the big bed' or 'the small doll'. Always speak in comparisons, for example, 'the biggest bed' or 'the smallest doll'. After all, a bed is only big if it is compared with other beds. It is best to keep dolls' clothes in a chest of drawers with a drawer for each of the three sizes, biggest, middle and smallest clothes, or different drawers for underwear, shirts, trousers, dresses and so on.

Both picture labels and written labels should be used on the drawers. The written labels need to be next to the pictures. If children can look at the pictures on the front of each drawer they quickly learn which clothes belong in which drawer and they begin to make sense of print.

Props which are not heavily pre-structured are useful. Some children will be helped to pretend if there is an old non-working hair dryer, but real hand cream, hair gel and other lotions are so real that they don't offer scope for pretend play. But they do offer real experiences, and are best arranged somewhere outside the home area.

Play props should be triggers for the child's own play ideas. They should help children to pretend, moving further and further from real life to more and more imagined situations.

Some children quickly learn to improvise and transform objects into play props, for example, a rolling pin might become a hair brush.

Some children do not need a prop at all and will mime brushing the hair.

Sand and water play

Mixing sand and water opens up opportunities for rich play places.

On the other hand, the Froebel Blockplay Research Project 1989–1992 found that although blockplay and small world play work well together, it is also important to value each in its own right.

There should be separate sand and water areas, and there is also a need for an area in the middle where the two can come together. It is important to consider carefully where to place the sand and the water. It is usual to put sand and water in commercially produced and very expensive trays. These are often on a stand with wheels.

A student from Greece on an early childhood education course in the UK was shocked by this. She was used to seeing children playing on a beach. A beach setting gives children opportunities for:

> ▶ dry sand play
> ▶ wet sand play
> ▶ water play
> ▶ making mixtures out of pebbles, shells and bits of seaweed with sand and water.

Water play

It is possible to create similar natural sand and water experiences for children in an indoor early childhood group setting with a large non-slip mat on the floor, with a mound of dry sand on it. There can be a commercial water tray in its stand next to this, and an empty tray or baby bath on the ground for mixing sand and water. Buckets can be placed around the edge of the mat. One can contain pebbles (large enough not to be swallowed). Another can contain twigs and other natural items such as leaves and fir cones. Another can hold play people. Another can have cartons to scoop water and sand with, and there can be one with lumps of plasticine. There can also be spades and buckets around the edge of the mat.

If children have not experienced this sort of play place before, they can easily be helped into it by adults who have been on the beach. Plasticine can be made into boats, as can cartons.

Play scenarios may develop with the play people going down the water chute, which can be made out of a piece of plastic guttering. The mound of dry sand can become mountains or can have a pond made in it by using a plastic yoghurt carton to stop the water draining through the sand.

Again, it is often best not to teach play techniques directly. Telling a story with the children sitting around the sand and water tray, while the adult has the area to create the story in, is a very powerful method for teaching children. Someone might be on a boat in the water tray, fall out, be rushed down a waterfall (the plastic guttering) into the muddy wet sand tray. They might make a house there and then walk to the dry mound of sand and climb a mountain. They might be thirsty and find a lake full of water to drink from.

Children from four to eight years of age will positively grab at ideas like this which they learn about in stories told to them by adults. They will use these ideas in their play. Younger children might need a much more everyday theme for their story, for example going for a walk and falling in a puddle (which could be the water tray), walking in the mud (the wet sand tray), and then walking along dry paths (the dry sand on the mat) and going home.

This kind of indirect teaching is very effective. In the Froebel Blockplay Project it was found that children gathered ideas in this way and often used them at a later time in their pretend play.

Children learn to think scientifically in this kind of play. Again, transforming things is important, just as it is in the home area. Children learn what is involved in transforming dry sand to wet sand. They learn that water, like dry sand, can be poured. They learn that wet sand is different in the way it behaves. Knowing about transformations is one of the most important areas that a scientist needs to think about.

This kind of sand and water play is easy to clear away. The buckets can be put on shelves at the end of the session. The mat can be rolled up and put, with the dry sand in it, under a table, or poured into the emptied water tray until the next day. It is unlikely that adults will want to provide this kind of sand and water play in this particular way every day.

Sometimes there might be a water tray set up with water pumps, and plastic squeezy bottles, containers with holes punctured in the sides. The children can see the water spurt out with more pressure at the bottom than at the top. Gradually children will begin to understand why divers need a diving bell to protect them from the pressure of the water when they dive deep into the sea.

There is always the need for plenty of containers and sieves and nets so that children learn that water goes through holes. There need to be opportunities to stop water from flowing, for example stoppers in plastic bottles, corks, or barriers on lock gates (commercially produced canal systems with locks are now available).

Watching children at water play, there will usually be some children who simply are learning about what water does and how it behaves. They might be fascinated by the way water goes through a sieve or colander. There will be other children who are playing with the water through pretend scenarios. For example putting a plastic play person in the water and making a plastic shark chase them, or escaping from it. These chase and catch and escape scenes are very strong and often seen when children play. These scenes become more and more elaborate as the children learn more and more about the possibilities.

Block area

Blockplay has always been an important tradition in early childhood. Some famous people have had wooden blocks to play with during childhood, and the impact of this childhood blockplay shows clearly in their adult lives. (See chapter 1.)

Blocks are best if they are wooden and are free standing. This means they do not connect with each other in the same way as a construction kit does. There are some large plastic construction kits on the market which are often mislabelled blocks. Because they connect with each other, they are construction kits and not free-standing blocks.

Blocks are difficult to play with if they are in a traffic route through which people walk frequently. Blocks need to be in a corner, in their own space on a firm, even floor. Tables wobble too much, and carpet with a thick pile is very frustrating because the blocks continually fall over.

Blocks need to be carefully presented to children. Preferably, they should be arranged on a shelf which has an outline for each type of block to be stored.

They can be stored in a box, but it can be difficult for a child to find the very block that is wanted if this slips to the bottom out of sight.

There need to be enough blocks. It is important that there is a complete set available all the time. Having a cylinder from one set, and finding that it is smaller than cylinders from another set, is very frustrating to a child trying to build with blocks. It makes children give up trying to play. Sets of blocks are like jigsaw puzzles. They need to be complete or children lose out on the play.

It is best to invest in one type of block which can be added to by buying supplementary sets. Wooden unit blocks are probably the most versatile to start with. In one nursery the staff had a long-term plan. They gradually bought three complete sets and added some supplementary sets. This took several years because blocks are expensive to buy. They then began to buy several sets of hollow blocks. These are larger and they had to plan the room so that there was sufficient space for them to be used. They then saw in a catalogue that there were mini-hollow blocks. They began buying these. Over a period of five years they had made a play space which offered a very rich variety of blockplay, using these three basic sets. All these sets, produced by the same manufacturer, related to each other mathematically. Children could use the sets separately, or together. In this nursery, the blockplay was of a very deep quality.

Sand, water and clay are relatively cheap to provide compared with wooden blocks and construction kits. On the other hand, buying a set of wooden blocks means you are investing in a valuable play prop which will last for thirty years or more.

Outdoor play

Children need space to run and leap about, to rough and tumble, to roly poly, to jump and land safely. The British Association for Early Childhood Education (BAECE) have found that children as young as three and four years old are in danger of developing heart disease because of few possibilities for outside play. Children attending nurseries with no outdoor space are at risk, especially if they watch television when they go home, and have no chance for large movement and play in a park (Jane Franklin, 1995).

Pretend play – football (the day after the European match England v. The Netherlands). Children need space to run about

Climbing frames need to be carefully designed to offer children plenty of challenges as safely as possible. One side of the frame might have evenly spaced rungs for children less experienced in climbing. Another side might have unevenly spaced rungs which need more thinking by the child.

An outdoor area needs some **tarmac** so that in wet weather it is possible to run or walk about without muddy feet tramping back indoors. It also needs **grass** which is used on finer days. Then children can find worms, make daisy chains and blow dandelion clocks.

Many gardens now have a **wild area** which has plants which encourage butterflies, moths and birds. A bird table is a source of great interest.

Children who see wildlife use their discoveries in their play.

Steven (seven years) and Ann (six years) played butterflies one summer afternoon. They followed each other about, pretending to land on flowers and dancing. They had scarves as wings, which they held with their hands, and flapped their arms up and down.

Tom saw a robin and a wren and a blackbird. He played at making a nest out of mown grass. He was a blackbird and hopped (having observed how they do this carefully). He put balls of blue dough in his nest. He had even noted the colour of the blackbird's eggs when shown them in a book about birds.

In their play, children show us what they have been learning.

A **grassy slope** can also provide rough and tumble play and roly poly play possibilities on a fine day.

Paddling pools are suitable for fine days, and their design has improved over the years. Some collapse down into a triangle and are easy to move and erect, and are less likely to puncture. If a group of children use the pool, it is worth investing in a large one, which is designed to last for years.

There are cultural sensitivities with regard to children taking off their clothes when using a paddling pool. These issues need to be carefully discussed and agreed between staff and parents before introducing children to a paddling pool.

There need to be clear boundaries about splashing so that some children are not put off. Perhaps there need to be 'splashy times' at certain points when children who enjoy this can stay in the pool, and children who dislike it can leave. In this way children learn to respect each other's needs, whilst being protected from what frightens them. They learn that what frightens one person might be a pleasure and delight to someone else. Respecting each other's feelings is important here.

It goes without saying that adults must constantly supervise a paddling pool. There should always be towels at hand. Children should leave their clothes on chairs or mats near the pool, and not be allowed to stay in the water if they become cold.

Some outdoor areas providing **digging patches** and a **vegetable planting area**. Then children can dig in ways appropriate to their understanding. Younger children tend to dig, transport earth about, find worms and tip water into holes. Older children begin to understand the process of digging, planting, watering and growing. This shows in their play. They want to play farmers or gardeners, and the sand pit is often where they will choose to do this.

A **sand pit outdoors** needs to be covered with a tarpaulin or plastic cover. These can be heavy so it is worth trying to find a design that is easy for staff to take off and put on. If there are buckets and spades and other containers such as sieves, pipes and tip-up lorries, children have the possibility to play at being builders, for example. A larger outdoor sand pit encourages quality play.

Indoors, it is only possible to provide a small area, so the outdoor sand pit is very important in this respect. Very few children have the opportunity of playing on the beach regularly.

Bikes are a subject of debate by early years practitioners. They can encourage bullying by a group of children who always get to ride on them. Sometimes children will actively harass other children to try to stop them taking the bike or having a turn. They can be used to rush around endlessly in ways which do not seem useful to the child's development. They can be a hazard to other children who may be knocked over.

For this reason, many settings now provide carts or the kind of bikes which require two or three children to co-operate in order to move them along. These are very useful in encouraging children to relate and help each other so that they can become a team as they play.

However, bikes are not always banned. They can make a useful contribution if there is a special zone where they can be used. There need to be clear boundaries when children use bikes.

It is no longer thought that girls-only sessions are useful. (There was a fashion for these in the 1980s.) It is the way girls and boys or timid and adventurous children are encouraged to play together by adults that is important. Adults have an important role to play in helping children to respect and be sensitive to each other.

A remark from the adult such as 'Are you sure you are ready to get off, James? Mark will wait until you have had your turn. You know you need to wait for James, don't you Mark?' helps both children to see ways forward which are fair for both of them.

If bikes are to be provided there need to be several, as having only one bike will cause problems. Staff often make an obstacle course in the bike riding zone, or a street layout which encourages road play.

Alastair (four years) pretended to be a stunt rider and appreciated having the obstacle course as it enhanced his play.

Bikes show us that it isn't the equipment itself which is the problem. It is how we help the children to use it that matters.

Places for quiet play

Play takes many forms. Sometimes it is quite noisy. At other times it is quieter and calmer. Children need both kinds of play according to the mood and moment. At one time there was a fashion for creating quiet rooms in group settings. It is now thought more helpful to provide quiet areas within different parts of the indoor and outdoor space. For example, a corner where there is a dolls' house and small world materials will lend itself to quieter play. This is particularly well placed next to what is sometimes called a workshop area, where children can use found materials such as cardboard boxes, scraps of material, string, buttons and other items and make them into models and collages.

If an adult makes a doll out of pipe cleaners and elastic bands and scraps of material, children quickly begin to do the same. If adults make dolls in lots of different ways, then children do not gain the damaging idea that there is only one way to make a doll. This gives them the confidence to try out different ways of doing things. Children will scavenge about and create the characters that they want to have in their small world play. It gives them more control over their small world play.

Being quiet sometimes makes adults believe that children are learning better than when they are noisy. In fact children learn well in both ways if their play shows that they are deeply involved in what they are doing.

Alistair was using the bike roughly, and was likely to break it. However, when the obstacle course was intro- duced, although his play was still noisy, he was able to pretend to be a stunt man (his father was a stunt man in films) and this helped him to have more focus in his play.

Summary

▶ Places to play can be made by arranging furniture and boxes, for example, under tables.

▶ Places to play need to be full of variety, for example, the home area, sand and water area, block area, paddling pools.

▶ The way we help children to use an area will be the key factor in determining whether or not there will be quality play, for example, the use of bikes in the playground.

▶ Quiet play is not superior to noisy play. The important thing is how involved the child is in the play.

7

Toys and Play Props

Toys

Toys are cultural artefacts.

This means that toys introduce children to some of the ideas that are important in the culture in which they are growing up. Many modern toys are designed so that they break easily, and yet they are often expensive. Some of the less reputable toy manufacturers almost seem to exploit the worries that parents (and grandparents) have about whether or not they are good enough parents if they do not buy the latest fashion in toys. There is a great emphasis on the idea that toys should teach a child to think, especially about reading, writing, numbers or science and technology.

These pre-structured toys are often labelled 'educational' or 'teaching toys' by commercial manufacturers. However, in fact they can hold back a child's education. For example, a telephone that talks when a child dials a number means that children quickly learn what the voice will say, and once they have listened a few times, they lose interest. In contrast, a simple non-speaking toy telephone encourages children to make up their own conversations with any topic of conversation and any characters they want to pretend.

The same applies to walkie talkie dolls that say 'mamma'. Supposing the child is pretending to be daddy? It spoils the child's play theme.

Pre-structured toys are designed to be used in highly specific ways. Often they are supposed to 'teach' children, for example to stack cups from large at the bottom to small at the top. However, children often use them quite differently from the way the designer intended, and bits quickly go missing.

Krister Svensson of the Centre for Research on Toy and Educational Media at the University of Halmstad in Sweden found that Swedish children in his research study have in their bedrooms an average of about 760 objects which the researcher labelled as 'toys'.

It is useful to look at traditional toys which have been loved and used by children in a rich variety of cultures across the world often for many centuries. Examples of these invaluable toys, which can be played with in an infinite number of ways, include: dolls, rag dolls, teddies, wooden blocks (bricks), dolls' houses and furniture, farm sets, road sets, a bat and balls, hoops, spinning tops, trucks.

The fascinating thing is that these are found in Museums of Childhood going back in time and also in many different cultures across the world. All of these toys can be used in very flexible ways. They encourage children to think, have ideas, and be imaginative as well as to sort out their feelings and relationships with other people.

Plastic toys and wooden toys

There are certainly some quality modern plastic toys, such as Duplo and Lego or Meccano. However, children need to experience natural materials as well in order to learn about the properties of wood, clay, mud, water, sand, as well as plastic and metal.

It is very important that toys are capable of being used flexibly by children. The problem with the way that many traditional toys have been used is that some are seen to be suitable only for girls (for example, dolls) whilst others are seen as suitable for boys (for example, toy cars).

Gender issues are an important consideration. In the last twenty years, early childhood educators and parents have worked hard to encourage both boys and girls to play with traditional toys more flexibly through carefully researched designs. This means that children are encouraged to play more broadly than previously.

There are now many dolls which show the rich variety of ethnic groups and people with different kinds of disability. Toy wheelchairs, calipers, dolls with glasses and other aids are now available.

Play props

Children are often very good scavengers for props, once they get the idea that things can be transformed and change from reality. They can be helped to make progress in this if adults give examples of how an object could become a play prop. 'Do you need some money, Connie? Here you are,

Pretending – getting ready to go shopping

you could pretend these buttons are the money.' In this example, the buttons are a bit like real money.

Some children need much more realistic props than others.

Barbara (two-and-a-half years) was pretending to be Mummy. She looked at the cot with a teddy in it.	She said 'I need a baby.' She went to get the realistic looking baby doll.

Some children do not need a prop at all, as mentioned in chapter 6. They can mime instead.

'Here's your change,' says Raffat (seven years) when he is pretending to be the shopkeeper. He takes imaginary money out of the cash	box, and mimes counting it out and pretends to give it to the imaginary customer.

In co-operative play in groups, children often use props more than when they play alone. Everyone in the group uses play props.

Two families joined for a picnic one weekend. They sat by a stream. The adults were a brother, John and his wife, and his sister and brother-in-law. The children were two boys, Matthew (four years), David (two years), Joanna (six years) and Toby (four years). John asked his sister if she remembered playing cave people in the garden as a child. She did.

The children took up this idea. Before long, there were baskets woven from grass, spears made from sharpened sticks, pebbles being caught as pretend fish in the grass baskets and a pretend fire built of twigs. Although adults led the play, the children brought ideas too and no-one dominated.

The props were important in the play, especially for David, Matthew and Toby. For example, David needed the twigs to build the pretend bonfire. It was an afternoon to be treasured, which no-one can ever take away from them.

Dressing-up clothes as play props

Dressing-up clothes need to be very simple, and open to all sorts of possibilities. A basic cape, some basic hats and drapes and scarves, and shoes, belts and shirt or baggy trousers can help children to imagine they are all sorts of people.

A firefighter's hat is all that is needed for most children to take on this character. A drape can become a sari. A pair of high heeled shoes gives the suggestion of becoming an adult woman. A cape turns a child into Zorro or Red Riding Hood.

In contrast, expensive, commercially made sets of clothes are very pre-structured. They control the role that has to be taken. Fortunately, in practice, children rarely use them as they are intended. They often take one bit of the costume, for example a clown's trousers, and pretend they are a boy going to a party, or something relating to their play theme. It would save expense not to buy elaborate costumes, but instead to have a set of very basic dressing-up clothes.

Children make great use of long clothes (long skirts and trousers) which cover them up. They love capes and hats with brims. They often want costumes with frills. This is because they are building up their understanding of basic shapes and patterns and special relationships. They like belts because they enclose the waist.

It is important to have a variety of fastenings which give children experience of different ways of connecting clothes together, for example, zips, buttons, tying bows, velcro.

Looking at books of different costumes, including adult roles in the UK and clothes worn across cultures, reminds children of possibilities and encourages them to play with the dressing-up clothes.

Summary

Toys

> ▶ Toys reflect the culture in which the child is growing up.
> ▶ They introduce children to their culture.
> ▶ They should be made to last, and not break easily.
> ▶ They need to have flexible ways for children to play with them.
> ▶ Pre-structured toys do not give children many possibilities for their use, because they do not encourage the imagination or creativity to develop.
> ▶ Boys and girls should not be stereotyped into narrow roles. This can be avoided if toys are not labelled as toys suitable for girls and toys suitable for boys.

Play props

> ▶ Children turn everyday objects that they find into play props. The twig which the child finds in the garden might become a play prop. It might become a 'pencil' in a child's pretend play.
> ▶ Sometimes children make their own play props. For example, the dough might be made into cakes by the child and used to play with in the home area.
> ▶ Sometimes children mime props: a child mimes washing his or her hair and mimes using a hair dryer.
> ▶ Dressing-up clothes help children to move into pretend roles and themes.

8

The Rhythms of Play

Children do not play all the time

The trouble with play is that you never know when it is going to happen!
When children are playing they are at their deepest levels of learning, so it
would be unrealistic to expect them to play all the time. When children
are experiencing this kind of learning, they need all the support adults can
give. Indirect help is usually the best. Direct help often causes play to
evaporate.

Adults will spend much of their time creating good places for children to
play, and setting things up so as to encourage play. When play begins to
flow, adults need to be ready to give help. Play will not wait. It will quickly
be gone unless it is encouraged there and then.

When adults see children reaching this deep level of free flowing play, it
is worth dropping everything else and being 'all systems go' to help it along.

NOW! QUICK! BEFORE IT IS GONE!

Adults help play to flow by:

> ▶ protecting children's play from interference
> ▶ adding props
> ▶ talk and extending the role or theme with children

The timetable, routines and rhythms of the day in relation to play

Children need to have a predictable shape to the day and a predictable
environment. Otherwise they do not know what is happening to them.

They quickly feel insecure and lose all sense of control over their lives. This does not mean that there should be a rigid timetable. The important thing is to shape the day so that there is a pattern which is familiar to the children.

In a group setting

In a group setting this will revolve around:

> ▶ arriving
> ▶ being indoors and outdoors
> ▶ snacks and storytimes
> ▶ outings
> ▶ mealtimes
> ▶ rest times
> ▶ partings

At home

At home things will be a little different. Key events will be:

> ▶ getting up and having breakfast
> ▶ being at home
> ▶ going shopping
> ▶ helping in the house
> ▶ other meals and snacks
> ▶ TV times, phone calls
> ▶ going to sleep

For deep quality play to flourish, it is very important to think how to use the times which are in between. This means the times that are in between arriving and going home, in between meals and outings. The more tightly structured these times are, the less possibility there is for children to play and reach their deepest levels of learning.

A tightly structured timetable

This type of timetable expects certain and definite things of children at specific times.

8.30 am	Children arrive
9.00 am	Group time
9.30 am	Finger painting
10.00 am	Snacks sitting around a table
10.15 am	Drawing and puzzles at tables
10.45 am	Choosing time
11.15 am–11.30 am	Going outside
	Clearing up time
11.30 am	Preparing for lunch: toilet, washing, etc.
11.45 am	Lunch
12.30 pm	Rest or quiet story
1.00 pm	Outdoors
2.00 pm	Collage
2.45 pm	Clearing up time
3.00 pm	Story and songs
3.30 pm	Children begin to be collected to go home.

Within the constraints of this very structured timetable, children will only have the possibility to play for half an hour in the morning, and for an hour in the afternoon out of doors. In fact, it takes children quite a long time to move into play. Half an hour is unlikely to be long enough to get there. Some children might just be getting into deep play when they have to stop.

In this particular early years setting, the outdoor area was not set up in a way which encouraged children to play with quality. There were no dens, no props. There were only two bikes, a water tray with a sieve and a few yoghurt cartons in it and a sand tray with a few plastic buckets and spades. In this setting the quality of play was poor. Indeed, not much play could be seen. This means that the children in this setting were not learning at a deep level.

A less structured timetable

The aim of this timetable is to create a predictable environment in which children feel safe and can begin to play deeply.

8.30 am	Children arrive
	Adults welcoming children and talking to parents.
	Children choose to be indoors or outdoors and have a choice of activities.
from 9.00 am to 11.00 am	Healthy snacks are available in a corner of the room where an adult is on hand to help the children if they need it.
	Children choose what they do. Adults are supporting children in their choices and extending learning. They use their daily plans and long-term plans to do this. The staff plans are based on observations of the children and are adjusted daily. However, there are also long-term aims for the children's learning.
11.00 am	Group time. Adults begin to help children clear up, then gather their groups into their corners and tell stories (planned beforehand), sing songs (selected beforehand) as well as chosen by the children there and then.
11.30 am	Some children are collected. Others prepare for lunch: toilet, washing, etc.
11.45 am	Lunch
1.00 pm	The morning children are joined by the children attending in the afternoon. Staff greet children as they arrive. Again there is a choice of activities both indoors and outdoors for children.

	The same pattern as the morning is followed but there are some different activities which again are based on the staff observations of children.
2.30 pm	Clearing up time and group times with songs and stories.
3.00 pm	Children begin to be collected to go home.

Once a week, children can choose to go on a short outing, perhaps to buy ingredients for cookery at the shop. Everything indoors and outdoors is put there to help the children learn. This means that whatever a child chooses to do, he or she can learn from it. To play deeply, children have to be in the mood, and the day needs a flexible shape which makes play a possibility most of the time. Play does not flourish when a timetable is tightly controlled by adults all day.

In this setting, children have enough time to work their way into deep flowing play. They have time to:

▶ get in the mood for play
▶ play
▶ unwind from their play as it fades.

There are differences in play in the mornings, afternoons and evenings. The child who has been cooped up in a small flat during a rainy weekend often positively roars into the early years setting on Monday morning, and probably heads for the outdoor area! This child is not going to be in any state to play until calmer and able to become involved and focused. Given half an hour or so, play will very likely become possible.

Early childhood practitioners in the UK often report that children play more quietly in the afternoon, but do not always become as involved. This needs to be carefully researched, then more will be known about the different play rhythms of the day.

In the early evening play, just before going to sleep, children often seem to have an urgent need for wild rough and tumble play, pillow fights, chasing and catching, whoops of glee. In some families and cultures this is followed by a relaxing bath full of chat and pretend play with boats, bubbles and sinking objects, and then a calm and gentle time with a bedtime story.

> ▶ rough and tumble play
> ▶ followed by bath play
> ▶ followed by story

Where this pattern of going to bed is the cultural norm, it is important that children are not beyond themselves with tiredness when bedtime begins. Plenty of time needs to be allowed for going to bed. Some adults do not answer the phone so they can give the children undivided attention. In modern life, sadly it is often the case that children are rushed to bed by tired adults who have been working all day.

In many cultures there is no such thing as 'bedtime'. Children go to sleep on an adult's lap or go to bed when adults do. Nevertheless, children still seem to indulge in rough and tumble play followed by a quieter time before going to sleep.

The rhythms of play vary, morning, afternoon and evening. Children have to be in the mood for play. A tired, hungry or sick child finds it hard to play. Adults can help play to flourish by shaping the day flexibly, whilst making sure that regular meals and quieter moments re-energise children.

Summary

> ▶ In order to play, the mood and moment must be right for children.
> ▶ Play can happen at any time, morning, afternoon or evening.
> ▶ Adults need to be ready to help it along when they see it.
> ▶ A timetable tightly controlled by adults does not help children to play.
> ▶ A day with a predictable shape and with flexible rhythms does help children to play.

9

Observing and Assessing Play

Observing play

Watching children at play is great fun, and very rewarding. It helps adults to
respect children and enjoy being with them. Parents can do this all the time,
and adoring grandparents absolutely delight in it. Children are the future of
our planet, and our greatest resource for survival.

Since play shows children at their deepest levels of learning, it is important
to use a structured way of observing it.

Assessing play

To assess whether children are developing well, and learning as much as
possible, carefully recorded observations of their deepest moments of play
must be kept. Since it is not possible, as we saw in the last chapter, to predict
when these 'high moments' will occur, we have to be ready to observe
when they do arrive. We need to ask colleagues to help in making this
possible. The whole team needs to make the observation of play a priority.

It goes without saying that a high staff ratio is of central importance. In some
reception, Year 1 and Year 2 classes in primary schools in England and
Wales, there are as many as 35–40 children with only one teacher. Research
at Goldsmiths College (1995) shows that teachers are often helped by an
untrained assistant. The teacher may not have trained to work with the
youngest children.

Young children are much more dependent for their physical, social,
emotional and intellectual needs than older children. They need warm,
close, consistent relationships, with staff who are trained in understanding
how young children develop and learn.

Even in this type of situation, which is unsuitable for children 4–7 years of
age, there are teachers who have the courage to encourage their children in
play and who take time for the observation of play. These teachers will be

better able to assess how deeply the children in the class are learning. Play tells adults about the depth of a child's learning.

Guidelines for observing play

It is extremely important not to make value judgements about a child's play. An example of this would be when an adult says a child is involved in noisy play, boisterous play, purposeless play. This is expressing an opinion. This type of statement should be challenged by colleagues, parents or Inspectors.

Instead, it is best to describe exactly what is happening. It is important not to analyse or interpret whilst making the observation: if you do this you are likely to start making value judgements and distorting what is happening.

The analysis or interpretation comes after the observation has been recorded.

> ▶ OBSERVATION: describe the context and what the child does and says
> ▶ ANALYSIS: analyse the observation to think about play and look at your observation with a play focus

Sometimes a chart can be useful for recording observations (see p. 71). With practice, people develop their own ways of making observations and assessments (Harding and Meldon–Smith, 1996). It is important simply to write down what you see the child say and do. It is best to target one child and to include specific detail of what that child says (Bartholomew and Bruce, 1993).

If you want to add anything to the observation, which seems to be important afterwards, then it is important to do this in a different coloured ink (for example, red ink). Always write the basic on-the-spot observation in a different colour. Then you can see which is:

> ▶ the on-the-spot observation
> ▶ the anecdotal (remembered afterwards) observation

Analysing the observation

In order to analyse your observation, use the indicators for play from chapter 2. Look at your observation. Now see if play indicator one is present. Do

Observing Play

Child's name:

Date of birth:

Date of observation:

Start time:

Finish time:

The Context	What the Child Says (if anything)	What the Child Does
The context in which the observation takes place, e.g. at the sand tray or in the garden or the tree.	*It is not always possible to write down everything word for word, but to get a few sample sentences completely written down is invaluable. If the child is not using English as his or her first language, you can use dashes to show whether the child seems to be using sentences or little phrases or single words.*	*Write down exactly what the child does without any judgement. Include the smallest aspects of behaviour.*

this with each play indicator. If there are seven or more of the play indicators present in your observation of a child's play, then it is likely that deep quality play is there.

If only a few of the play indicators are present, it does not mean the child is not learning, it probably means that the child is using a different strategy for learning. For example, a game, representation or a first-hand experience.

Alternatively, it may mean that the child

> ▶ is young and so has yet to develop symbolic aspects of play
> ▶ is challenged in some way and so needs particular help in developing his or her play

At the end of the recording write a few sentences which summarise what you now know about the child's play.

Examples

BOBBIE (SIX MONTHS)

Bobbie is sitting propped up with cushions behind and beside him. He has a basket of objects in front of him – a wooden spoon, metal key, cork, thick china saucer, matching cup.

He picks up the spoon, wrapping his left hand round the handle. He transfers it to his right hand. He twists the spoon, and looking at it intently puts it in his mouth. He can only get the tip in his mouth. He chews the edge of the spoon, still holding the handle. He bounces up and down on his bottom, on the spot, smiling and saying 'bah, bah' several times. He looks around as he bounces using his heels to lever his bottom up and down on the spot. He is still holding the spoon in his right hand. He stops bouncing and looks at the spoon again. He looks again, puts it in his mouth and chews it. He again bounces on his bottom, looks around and smiles and says 'bah, bah'.

The following play indicators are present:

1. Bobbie is using direct first-hand experiences of the spoon.
2. He has made his own rules. These consist of a little sequence, a pattern which he repeats: bounce, smile, suck the spoon, say 'bah, bah'.

4. No-one is making him do things.
7. He is alone.
9. He has his own play agenda. This means he has his own ideas about what he wants to do.
10. He is deeply involved in what he is doing and is difficult to distract.
11. He is showing his latest skills at grasping objects, sitting, and being able to bounce up and down without falling over from the sitting position.
12. He is co-ordinating and bringing together his feelings ('bah, bah' and smiles), his ideas (about using a spoon) and his relationship (he looks at me watching and smiles).

Bobbie is at the beginning of playing. Seven of the play indicators are there. His play has yet to use symbols. This means he is not yet using something or a person to stand for objects and people. He does not represent. He does not rehearse a role. He does not pretend. He does not have a play theme. This will be the next exciting development in his play.

SUKVINDER (18 MONTHS)

Sukvinder toddles straight across the flower bed in the garden, pushing a pram full of plastic cups and saucers, beads, and yoghurt cartons. She continues across the grass on to the tarmac and stops at the sand-pit. She takes out one cup. She drops it in the sand-pit. She repeats this with various objects, beads, plates, saucers, more cups. Then she picks up some of the objects she has put in the sand-pit one by one (those nearest to her). She leaves some. She walks off pushing them along, transporting them to the home area.

She stops and then takes out many of the objects (those nearest to her hands it seems) and once it is empty she begins as before to refill it, using some of the objects she has taken out. She drinks from the cup (or pretends to).

The following play indicators are present:

1. She is directly using first-hand experience of what cups and saucers are for, and prams to push things about.
2. She has her own rules about stopping and starting, putting in and taking out. This is a pattern.
4. No-one is making her do this.
6. She pretends to drink from the cup.
7. She is alone.

10. She is deeply involved in her ideas, feelings and relationships with other children and adults.
11. She shows what she knows about pushing and what she does not know about understanding flower beds and drinking from the cup.
12. She is bringing together and co-ordinating different areas, spacial understanding (in out, transporting and symbols), for example, a pretend drink from a cup.

Sukvinder is using symbols in her play. Eight of the play indicators are present. She can only very fleetingly pretend to drink out of a cup. She does not yet take on role-play or rehearse for adult life. She does not yet have a play theme.

However, pretend play is a huge development. Adults will need to encourage it.

MAURICE (THREE YEARS), JADE (THREE YEARS)

Maurice and Jade are making a den under the table in the kitchen in Jade's home. Jade goes to the kitchen cupboard and takes out all the tins. The two children carry them to their den and put them in a row inside.

'This can be our food, can't it?' says Maurice.

'Yes. Let's have supper, darling,' says Jade. Jade pretends to open a tin and scoop the food out. 'This can be the cooker,' says Maurice, using an old box he finds outside the den. They pretend cook and then pretend eat. They are moving into symbolic play.

The following play indicators are present:

1. They use their experiences of real life – but not directly, because they are remembering what it is like to cook and eat at a table rather than being in a real situation.
2. They are making their own rules together. This box shall be a cooker. These tins shall be our food.
4. They are not made to do this.
5. Jade talks to Maurice as if they are adults. Perhaps he is her husband: 'darling'. Here is the beginning of role-play and rehearsal for adult life.
6. Both children are pretending.
8. They play co-operatively together.

9. They have a play theme: houses and eating meals.
10. They are deeply involved in it.
11. They try out what they know about cooking and eating together.
12. Their play is co-ordinating what they do, bringing together different areas of thinking, feelings and relationships.

Here we have deep quality play. Nine play indicators are present for Maurice. Although he is pretending, he is not using role-play. Ten play indicators are present for Jade, who is.

JASON (FOUR YEARS), SHARON (FIVE YEARS), TRACEY (FOUR YEARS), EMILY (SIX YEARS)

Jason and Emily are brother and sister. The children often play in each other's houses. They have done so since they were babies. Jason has a mild learning disability and mild behavioural disorders.

Emily suggests they play rainforests. She has seen a programme about Indians living in the rainforests of Brazil on television. She suggests they make a village.

They all make a den together in the garden, scooping up grass cuttings from the recently mown lawn. They put these in a heap to mark a wall for a den. Jason becomes absorbed in doing this but he keeps putting his scoops of grass into a bucket he finds. He tips the bucket into the den.

'No!' shouts Tracey. 'You are spoiling our village.'

'I know,' says Emily, 'that can be the food we cook on our fire.'

Jason throws the next bucket load in another part of the den.

'Oh, he is spoiling our village!' cries Tracey. 'Stop it, Jason!'

Emily says, 'Jason, only put it here. Look. Jason, put it here. You can be the man who brings the food, but you must only put it here. Look, when you bring the food I am the Chief. I say "put it here" and you do it, because I am the Chief, and you have to do what I say.'

Jason laughs. He waits for her to say 'put it here' and then runs away to scoop up more grass.

Tracey is the child who stays in the village. Sharon goes off and collects food like Jason. She finds a teddy and brings it back, but she does not take it inside the den. She says 'This is the goat. I am milking the goat. The goat has to stay outside, doesn't he?'

Emily says 'Yes, and the Chief comes and says bring me some milk.' The play flows along.

These play indicators are present in the group play:

1. Although the theme came from a television programme, the children had a rich variety of real experiences which meant that the programme about rainforests acted as an enhancer to real experience.
2. The children were constantly making their own play rules. Grass became food. Grass became walls of the village house. Teddies became goats.
4. No-one made them do this.
5. Emily, Tracey and Sharon were taking on adult roles. Jason was not.
6. Emily, Tracey and Sharon were pretending. Jason was not. He was enjoying scooping, transporting and throwing grass into piles.
7. Jason was playing alone.
8. Emily and Sharon were playing co-operatively. Tracey was playing associatively.
9. There was a clear play theme: 'rainforests'. Within that, Sharon wanted to scoop up grass and milk goats. Tracey wanted to be a child in the house. Emily was the Chief. Emily's theme was the most elaborate, but she knew how to simplify it and make it manageable for the other children, who did not know as much about rainforests and the people who live in them.
10. All the children were deeply involved.
11. All the children were showing their skills. Jason managed not to disrupt the play, helped by Emily. Both children sensed it was important, since none of the children wanted the play to stop.
12. The children were all co-ordinating different things they knew about, ideas, feelings and relationships.

In this group play, eleven out of the twelve play indicators are present. The children had plenty of time to move into play. They had the whole afternoon. The play flowed for about two hours. It ended abruptly when Jason threw the bucket at Tracey, who cried, and Emily had to fetch an adult into the garden.

John Paul (four years), Shanine (four years)

John Paul made a model out of boxes. He said it was an aeroplane. 'It's a bomber,' he said. He took his model aeroplane from the table, and ran about the playground making aeroplane noises and the sound of bombs dropping. Shanine quickly made an aeroplane too. She rushed to join John Paul. The children put stones from the tarmac on top of their aeroplanes, and as they ran about the stones dropped off as the bombs.

The adult supervising the play had no idea that the children had a war play theme. What she saw was two children rushing about flying aeroplanes. When they started flying their aeroplanes near other children, she intervened because she could see they were upsetting some of the children by doing this. One of the children told the adult about the stones being bombs. The teacher said that war play was not allowed and they must stop this play.

The following play indicators are present:

1. John Paul and Shanine were using what they know about aeroplanes. They do not have any real experience or knowledge of bombs except through watching television. They linked bombs with objects falling from a great height and making a noise when they land.
2. They are making up their own rules. Boxes are turned into aeroplanes. Stones are turned into bombs.
3. They are using their representations (their model aeroplanes) as play props.
4. No-one has made them do this.
6. They are pretending the boxes are aeroplanes and the stones are bombs.
8. They are playing co-operatively.
9. The adult does not respect this play theme. The adult stops the play.
10. The children were deeply involved.
11. They were trying out what they knew about dropping objects from a height, but had difficulty hitting a target.
12. They were co-ordinating different ideas, feelings and relationships.

Ten of the twelve play indicators are present in this observation. The play raises the difficult issue of war play. Obviously the children's play cannot be left as it is. However, an adult joining the play might help children to sort out the implications and effects of war. Because adults find war repugnant does not mean that young children should not be allowed to think about it. In fact the research shows that when children are helped to do so in their play, they think more deeply about what wars mean. What will the pilot and crew eat? Where will they sleep? Emphasise the pain of being hurt, and the cause and effect aspect.

Judy Dunn (1988) and Carlsson-Paige and Levin (1990) suggest that helping children to develop and elaborate such play might help children to develop morally much more effectively than simply banning this kind of play. It helps children to think about the effect when bombs are dropped, and the loss of human lives, and what this means to families. However, adults usually ban play themes which they do not like. This is a difficult issue and adults tend to have very strong feelings about it.

Observing and assessing play

Three of these examples were in home situations. Inspectors often report that they see a dismal picture of poor quality play in reception and Year 1 and 2 classes in primary schools. This is not the case in nursery schools. It is very important that adults working with young children are able to recognise and assess quality play. It is also important that they are able to monitor a child's progress in play, and know how to help children learn through their play.

There is progression in play in these observations of Bobbie, Sukvinder, Maurice, Jade, Jason, Sharon, Tracey and Emily.

If only a few of the play indicators are present, adults should see where help is needed and consider the next step for the child's progress in play. No-one would expect Bobbie to be using symbols at six months. However, as he sees older brothers and sisters, friends and parents pretend playing, it shows him possibilities, which in time he can use. He might use it as young as a year or so in age, according to Judy Dunn (1988).

If a child has been deprived of enriching first-hand experiences, this will be a priority as it is the bedrock of play. Adults working with children with special educational needs concentrate on the importance of first-hand experience as the first step in encouraging play. This is particularly so when working with children with severe challenges (RNIB video series, 1995).

Baseline assessment of play

There is a great deal of discussion about baseline testing or assessment of children before they have reached the age of five. It is helpful to remember that 'baseline' means 'starting point'. This means adults need to know how a child plays when first joining a group. It is then possible for adults to monitor the child's progress in the way he or she plays.

The observation and assessment techniques in this chapter can be used to make a baseline assessment of a child's play. It is best to do this during the very first week of the child starting in the group otherwise it will not be a baseline assessment (Bartholomew and Bruce, 1993).

Once the child is settled, it is possible to see the progress in the play. This can be done by monitoring or recording the child's play progression by regularly observing the child at play, both alone and with other children and adults.

Using observation to inform the way the curriculum is planned

This will be considered in the next chapter, which is about how to offer a quality curriculum to young children. Observations help adults to assess the quality and progress a child makes when playing. Observations also need to be used to inform the adult about the next step in the child's learning, and to develop curriculum plans.

Summary

> ▶ When observing play it is important to avoid value judgements and opinions. Instead there should be a description of what the child says and does, and the context in which the play takes place.
> ▶ The play can be assessed and analysed through using the twelve indicators for play (see chapter 2).
> ▶ Inspectors in primary schools (not nursery schools) have expressed their concern about the quality of play that they find. This means that the quality of learning is being constrained for many young children, especially those in reception classes and in Years 1 and 2 of the primary school in England and Wales.
> ▶ Structured observations of a child's play need to be made regularly in order to assess:
>   – the baseline or starting point when the child joins the group
>   – the progress the child makes in his or her play

The Early Childhood Curriculum and Play

Planning the curriculum for play

The curriculum has three areas.

THE THREE Cs OF THE EARLY CHILDHOOD CURRICULUM

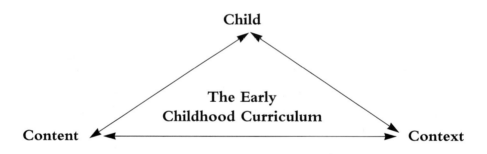

Child

**The Early
Childhood Curriculum**

Content   **Context**

What the child already knows

What the child needs to know

**What the child wants to know
more about**

**People, culture, race, gender,
special educational needs,
access, materials and physical
environment, outdoors,
indoors, places, events**

In thinking about how the curriculum relates to play, it is possible to use different chapters from this book.

The child

The child was the focus of chapters 1 and 2.

THE CHILD IN CONTEXT

However, the child must always be seen as the **child in context**.

Chapters 3, 4 and 5 emphasised the way in which adults can help children to play by creating a context which encourages play.

Chapters 6, 7 and 8 focused on material provisions and making time for play.

Chapter 9 looked at the importance of adults observing and assessing play.

When helping children to play it is important to think about these two aspects:

> ▶ people who help children to play
> ▶ provision that helps children to play

THE CONTENT

What children learn through play is the subject of this chapter. Children in Years 1 and 2 of key stage 1 are required to follow the National Curriculum in the UK. The areas of learning which follow are those suggested for children in reception and other settings working with children until they are five years of age. They go beyond the minimal requirements of the Ofsted/SCAA document 'Desirable Outcomes' 1996.

Language and literacy

Children need opportunities to talk and listen to each other and adults. This is often a central aspect of play and later becomes improvisation in drama. The home area is an excellent way of encouraging storying (which has a theme and characters). This later becomes creative writing. Telephone directories, appointment books, recipe books and so on are all part of the linguistic and literary aspects of play. They all encourage play in relation to writing and reading.

It might be useful to look again at the home area and see whether this has opportunities which encourage linguistic and literary learning.

It is also important to remember that the stories you read aloud to or tell children using props, puppets and pictures will have a great impact on the child's play themes. Many children will only be able to use television themes (such as cartoons) if they do not have stories told to them.

Having book areas and graphics areas with pens, pencils and paper dotted about the room and in dens in the outside areas also encourages children to use books for stories and for finding things out and reference. As children browse through books they find play ideas, which help to enrich their play.

Adults who observe what children do will be in a better position to use their observations to inform the way they set up different areas. For example, the home area can be set up to enhance the needs of individual children, as well as serving the needs of children in general.

Mathematics

Some areas lend themselves to mathematical play more than others. That is why it is so important to include a rich variety of play props for children.

Again, the home area encourages play involving mathematical ideas. So does a set of wooden blocks, water or sand play. Ideas about space, time, shape and size, patterns, weight, number, area, links, volume and capacity, all come into mathematical play.

The child who crouches and walks around pretending to be a toddler, as small as possible, holding the hand of an upright child who is pretending to be an adult, is showing an understanding of the comparative heights of adults and children. A child is shorter than an adult.

Mathematics is everywhere, and it will be part of a child's play. It is worth looking out for it so that children can be helped to extend their mathematical thinking.

Aesthetics

TWO AND THREE-DIMENSIONAL ART

Play can be seen whilst children draw, paint, print, weave, make collages, sew, do woodwork, sculpture, or pottery. However, very often these kinds of materials lead children into representation more than play. In other words, children very often make a product to be kept.

But they do not always do this. Very young children might make something and keep changing it as their play ideas flow along. A hand print in finger painting might at one moment be a chestnut leaf, then a peacock's fanned tail, then a spider. Children do not always want to make a representation or a product that they can keep. If they do, it might be used as a play prop rather than put on a shelf or pinned on a wall for a display.

MUSIC

Children often use sounds and songs as they play. 'Brm, brm' is the familiar roar of an engine. Cats are heard miaowing for milk, baby voices are pitched high. Children learn about pitch, loudness and how to make musical sounds and melodies and this shows in their play.

The Desirable Outcomes curriculum document calls these areas creative development, but children can be creative in all areas of development.

Knowledge and understanding of the world

Natural science (animals, birds, reptiles, fish, mini-beasts and plants) needs a garden. Children deprived of play in a garden are less likely to play scientifically or technologically. Playing at being birds in a nest, rabbits in a burrow, spiders in their webs, shows what children know and understand about these aspects of natural science. In their play, children show us what they know about science and technology in creative ways.

The physical sciences and low technology and high technology are important for children to learn in modern life. Playing at making omelets with an egg whisk is technological play. Pretending people are in a sandstorm in a desert and using dry sand sprinkled on wet sand in the sand area shows that children know about the properties of sand and water and how it will behave.

Children often play 'old fashioned times' and dress up in clothes with long skirts, cloaks and so on. They also often play people who live somewhere else, such as a jungle, forest, on a lake, up a mountain. How people live in other places and how people used to live are the beginnings of interest in history and geography. Play offers children large opportunities to show what they know about these areas of knowledge and understanding.

It is important to return to the basic principle that when adults are careful observers of children's play they can use these observations to help plan the curriculum.

Physical development

Children move about as they play. They use large apparatus such as climbing frames and small apparatus such as bats and balls. They use space outside, especially to run, jump, roll, skip and hop. Given the opportunity, they swim and try out dances.

> Josh and Sally, both four-year-olds, ran forwards and both put the toes of one foot out. They waved their foot and screamed. They ran backwards laughing. They repeated this. This was a dance sequence which they were using in their play. They kept changing what they did every few minutes.

The next day an adult asked them if they would repeat it. They couldn't. It had been a moment of play, and play is not meant to last. It had faded.

Personal and social development

In their play, children show that they are thinking about moral matters such as being physically violent, what war means, kindness, justice and fairness. Play also brings them inner peace from frustration and emotional pain, and helps them to co-ordinate the things that they know. Friedrich Froebel (1782–1852) believed that play is the most spiritual activity of the child.

As they play, children think about kindness, justice and fairness, and they learn about self-control

USING OBSERVATIONS AND ASSESSMENT OF A CHILD'S PLAY TO PLAN THE CURRICULUM

It will only be possible to offer a quality early years curriculum if it is based on the observation and assessment of children. Before reading this chapter, it is necessary to read chapter 9 which looks at observing and assessing children. You will need to use the observations and assessments you make of children and their play in order to inform your curriculum planning.

Maria, five years old, is playing in the home area. She answers the telephone and pretends to talk to her friend. 'Yes. Come over for a cup of tea. That will be nice. See you soon.' She puts the phone down. The friend arrives and knocks on the door. She answers, and lets her in. She can't find any cups and saucers in the dresser. She goes to the phone and picks it up. 'Hello. Is that the shop? I need some more cups. Do you have some? Yes. Thank you. I will come to your shop now.'

She goes out of the house, leaving her friend. Her friend sits at the table for a while but then goes to the dough table where she begins to become involved in making pretend cakes. She does not return to the home area.

This observation can be used to inform the curriculum planning. It is likely that Maria's play would not have faded if there had been enough cups and saucers in the dresser. Her friend might have stayed with her. She would not have left the home area.

The home area needs to be checked so that it has crockery in it. There needs to be a team plan to discuss clear boundaries that the children can be given about removing crockery from the home area.

Maria needed support in her play. If an adult had quickly found some yoghurt cartons and arrived at the door saying they were the cups to be delivered from the shop, this might also have enabled Maria to keep her play flowing with her friend.

Adults could use this observation to plan as follows:

► reorganise equipment in the home area and have a policy about it which the children understand and the staff use confidently

▶ try to be there to support Maria as she moves into pretend play.
   She needs this in order to keep the play flowing
   a) the character (the role she was playing)
   b) the story (the theme she is playing)
▶ supporting her with her play role and her play theme will help
   Maria to learn about the linguistic and literary areas of knowledge.
   Both of these are important in creative writing and in reading
   literature. If there had also been a telephone book and notepad
   and a pencil beside the telephone, this would have helped Maria
   to elaborate her play through taking the role of someone writing
   and looking up information.

Summary

▶ A quality curriculum is based upon observation of children.
▶ It means observing a child playing and putting energy into creating
   a context for play to make progress. The context is made up of
   people as well as the physical environment, space and organisation
   of time.
▶ It means helping children to learn subjects as part of play. The
   subject areas are:
   – language and literacy
   – mathematics
   – aesthetic
   – creative
   – physical
   – personal and social
   – knowledge and understanding of the world.
▶ Observation of play informs the way the curriculum can be
   planned to help children be supported and to elaborate their play.

Conclusion

- ▶ A child who is helped to play is a child who is helped to develop and learn.
- ▶ In some cultures children are encouraged to play in schools and group settings.
- ▶ In some cultures play takes place outside these settings, with older brothers, sisters and friends teaching younger children how to play.
- ▶ The more that is learnt about children's play, the more it seems that play co-ordinates and brings together the developing and learning that children do. It helps children to sort out and make meaning of their lives.
- ▶ For children experiencing great stress, play does not develop so easily. This means that a powerful learning mechanism is breaking down and cannot be brought into use by the child without sensitive and skilled adult help.
- ▶ For most children, play flourishes if it is given half a chance. Perhaps this is because it is very central for human beings in their development and learning.
- ▶ Helping children to play is one of the most worthwhile and important things an adult can do.

Bibliography and References

Athey, C., (1990) Extending Thought in Young Children. A Parent–Teacher Partnership. London: Paul Chapman Publishing.

Axline, V., (1969) Play Therapy (rev. ed.). New York: Ballantine Books.

Bartholomew, L. and Bruce, T., (1993) Getting to Know You. A Guide to Record Keeping in Early Childhood Education and Care. London: Hodder & Stoughton.

Blenkin, G. and Kelly, V., (2nd ed) (1996) Early Childhood Education: A Developmental Curriculum. London: Paul Chapman Publishing.

Bruce, T., (1987) Early Childhood Education. London: Hodder & Stoughton.

Bruce, T., (1991) Time to Play in Early Childhood Education. London: Hodder & Stoughton.

Bruce, T., Findlay, A., Read, J., Scarborough, N., (1995) Recurring Themes in Education. London: Paul Chapman Publishing.

Bruce, T. and Meggitt, C., (1996) Child Care and Education. London: Hodder & Stoughton.

Bruner, J., (1990) Acts of Meaning. Cambridge M.A.: Harvard University Press.

Carlsson-Paige, N. and Levin, D.E., (1990) Whose Calling the Shots? How to Respond Effectively to Children's Fascination with War Play and War Toys. Philadelphia USA, Canada: New Society Publishers.

Davies, M., (1995) Helping Children to Learn through a Movement Perspective. London: Hodder & Stoughton.

Dunn, J., (1988) The Beginnings of Social Understanding. Oxford: Blackwell.

D.F.E.E., (1996) Desirable Outcomes for Children's Learning on Entering Compulsory Education. D.F.E.E./S.C.A.A.

Drummond, M.J., (1993) Assessing Children's Learning. London: David Fulton Publishers Ltd.

Erikson, E., (1963) Childhood and Society. London: Routledge and Kegan Paul.

Fein, G.G. (1981) Pretend Play: An Integrative Review. Child Development, 52, 195–1118.

Findlay, A., (1995). See Bruce, Findlay, Read and Scarborough.

Franklin, J., Education Today. British Council Issue 10, December 1995.

Freud, A., (1964) The Psycho-analytical Treatment of Children. N.Y. International University Press.

Froebel, F., (1887) The Education of Man. New York: Appleton.

Goldsmiths College, (1995) Diversity Project. Lewisham Way, London.

Gotberg, E., (1995) A Guide to Promoting Resilience in Children. Van Leer Foundation.

Groos, K., (1922) The Play of Man. New York: Appleton.

Gura, P., (ed) (1990) Exploring Learning: Blockplay in the Early Years. London: Paul Chapman Publishing.

Gura, P., (1996) Resources for Early Learning: Children, Adults and Stuff. London: Hodder & Stoughton.

Gussin Paley, V., (1981) Wally's Stories. Cambridge M.A. London: Harvard University Press.

Gussin Paley, V., (1984) Boys and Girls: Super Heroes in the Doll Corner. Cambridge M.A. London: Harvard University Press.

Gussin Paley, V., (1986) Mollie is Three. Cambridge M.A. London: Harvard University Press.

Gussin Paley, V., (1988) Bad Guys Don't Have Birthdays: Fantasy Play at Four. Cambridge M.A. London: Harvard University Press.

Gussin Paley, V., (1990) The Boy Who Would Be a Helicopter. The Uses of Story Telling in the Classroom. Cambridge M.A. London: Harvard University Press.

Gussin Paley, V., (1994) You Can't Say You Can't Play. Cambridge M.A. London: Harvard University Press.

Gussin Paley, V., (1995) Kwanzaa and Me. Cambridge M.A. London: Harvard University Press.

Harding, J. and Meldon-Smith, L., (1996) How to Make Observations and Assessments. London: Hodder & Stoughton.

Honig, A., (1984) 'Working in partnership with parents of handicapped infants'. Early Childhood Development and Care. 14, 1–2, pp. 13–36.

Hurst, V., (1991) Planning for Early Learning. London: Paul Chapman Publishing.

Isaacs, S., (1968) The Nursery Years. London: Routledge and Kegan Paul.

Klein, M., (1986) The Selected Melanie Klein. (J. Mitchell, ed.) London: Penguin.

Lally, M., (1991) The Nursery Teacher in Action. London: Paul Chapman Publishing.

Laidman, P., (1992) Accident Prevention in Day Care and Play Settings. NES, Arnold.

Matthews, J., (1994) Helping Children to Draw and Paint: Visual Representation. London: Hodder & Stoughton.

McMillan, M., (1930) The Nursery School. London: Dent.

Meade, A. with Cubey, P., (1995) Thinking Children. New Zealand Council for Educational Research. (Available from ABC Books, Isaac Newton Centre, Kensington, London).

Moyles, J., (ed) (1994) The Excellence of Play. Buckingham, Philadelphia, Open University Press.

Moyles, J., (1990) Just Playing? Buckingham, Philadelphia, Open University Press.

Neilsen, L., (1993) Step by Step. Sikon Press. (Available from RNIB, Garrow House, 190 Kensal Road, London W10 5BT).

Neilsen, L., (1992) Space and Self: Active Learning by Means of the Little Room. Sikon Press. (Available from RNIB, Garrow House, 190 Kensal Road, London W10 5BT).

O'Hagan, M. and Smith, M., (1993) Special Issues in Child Care. Baillière Tindall.

Opie, I. and Opie, P., (1988) The Singing Game. Oxford, NY: Oxford University Press.

Parten, M., (1933) Social Play Among Pre-School Children. Journal of Abnormal and Social Psychology, 28, 136–147.

Pascal, C. and Bertram, A., (eds) (1997) Effective Early Learning. London: Hodder & Stoughton.

Piaget, J., (1962) Play, Dreams and Imitation in Childhood. London: Routledge and Kegan Paul.

Rentoul Outhwaite, I., (1928) Blossom. London: A. & C. Black Ltd.

RNIB, (1995) Play it My Way. London: H.M.S.O.

Roberts, R., (1995) Self Esteem and Successful Early Learning. London: Hodder & Stoughton.

Rogers, C., (1983) Freedom to Learn for the 80s. N.Y.: Merrill-Macmillan.

Sylva, K., Appendix C. 'The Impact of Early Learning in Children's Later Development', in Ball, C., (1994, March) Start Right. The Impact of Early Learning. RSA 84–96.

Vygotsky, L., (1978) Mind in Society. Cambridge M.A.: Harvard University Press.

Winnicott, D.W., (1974) Playing and Reality. Harmondsworth: Penguin Books.

Whitehead, M., (1996) The Development of Language and Literacy. London: Hodder & Stoughton.

Whalley, M., (1994) Learning to be Strong: Integrating education and care in early childhood. London: Hodder & Stoughton.

Index